This Precious Life

This Precious Life

TIBETAN BUDDHIST TEACHINGS

ON THE PATH TO

ENLIGHTENMENT

Khandro Rinpoche

SHAMBHALA

Boston & London

2005

Shambhala Publications, Inc.
Horticultural Hall
300 Massachusetts Avenue
Boston, Massachusetts 02115
www.shambhala.com

9 8 7 6 5 4

Printed in the United States of America

∞ This edition is printed on acid-free paper that meets the
American National Standards Institute z39.48 Standard.
♻ Shambhala Publications makes every effort to print on recycled
paper. For more information please visit www.shambhala.com.
Distributed in the United States by Random House, Inc.,
and in Canada by Random House of Canada Ltd

*The Library of Congress catalogues the previous
edition of this book as follows*:
Rinpoche, Khandro.
This precious life: Tibetan Buddhist teachings on the path
to enlightenment/Khandro Rinpoche.
p. cm.
Includes bibliographical references and index.
ISBN 978-1-57062-307-3 (cloth)
ISBN 978-1-59030-174-6 (paper)
1. Spiritual life—Buddhism 2. Buddhism—Doctrines.
3. Buddhism—China—Tibet. I. Title.
BQ7604.R56 2003
294.374—DC21
2002014199

THIS BOOK IS DEDICATED

TO HIS HOLINESS MINDROLLING TRICHEN

AND MY MOTHER,

SANGYUM SONAM PALDRÖN

Contents

Contents

Foreword

W E ALL SEEK HAPPINESS and shun suffering, but as human beings we are distinguished from others by our intelligence. If we allow it to be controlled by negative emotions like hatred, the consequences are disastrous, but if we use it positively, we can not only recognize our predicament but also train our minds and ways of thinking, which enables us to transform ourselves into better, happier people. The Four Reminders, explained here, form the bedrock of Buddhist practice. They are intended to encourage us to make our lives meaningful, which we can do by developing a kind heart and a sense of love, compassion, and respect for others. Khandro Rinpoche, the author of this book, is a young Tibetan woman who has had the benefit of combining religious upbringing and training with modern education, which lends a refreshing contemporary clarity to her explanation.

His Holiness the Fourteenth Dalai Lama

ACKNOWLEDGMENTS

I wish to acknowledge Mindrolling Jetsun Dechen Paldron for her tireless effort, generosity, and wisdom. I would also like to mention Helen Berliner, without whom this book wouldn't have been possible; Eugenia Pickett, for her careful compilation and editorial input; and Dr. Karl Gross, for all his hard work and patience.

Editor's Preface

☉

THIS BOOK PRESENTS topics considered to be essential preliminaries to Buddhist practice and understanding. Central to this understanding, from the beginning to the end of the journey, are the Four Thoughts That Transform the Mind. These four contemplations—on the preciousness of human existence, impermanence, suffering, and karma—are sometimes called the Four Reminders and are considered to be transformative in and of themselves.

The first thought, the preciousness of a human life, is the unifying theme of this book. By virtue of our possessing a human birth, the cessation of suffering is possible and the gateway to liberation is open to us. Therefore, this human life is said to be precious. It is also said to be as fragile as a bubble, and this brings a sense of urgency to the path of practice—as well as a need to understand the infinitely creative ways we perpetuate suffering when, in fact, all sentient beings long for happiness. The book concludes with teachings on "entering the gateway," a traditional metaphor to describe taking refuge in the Three Jewels of Buddha, Dharma, and Sangha, the fruition of which is enlightenment and a genuine ability to benefit sentient beings.

All of the teachings presented here examine suffering and liberation in light of our innate human wisdom and goodness. They come to us by virtue of our great good fortune in this life— and through the extreme kindness and generosity of Khandro Rinpoche. A teacher dedicated to presenting the pure essence of

Tibetan Buddhism, Khandro Rinpoche illuminates this profound and practical path in such a way that it actually enables one to bring one's human life to fruition.

—*Helen Berliner*

Supplication

THE TRADITIONAL WAY to begin a text is to offer supplications and prayers to all the buddhas and bodhisattvas. It is *their* teachings that are being passed down to this moment through an unbroken lineage. This transmission is completely pure. By supplicating, we come to realize the tremendous responsibility we have as the containers into which the lineage is being transferred. Before receiving instructions that bring the mind to awareness, we have a valid reason to act out of ignorance. Having received such instructions, each of us is faced with a choice: we can choose to remain ignorant, or we can choose to work hard to develop something beneficial for ourselves and others. May this supplication form the basis for committing ourselves to exert effort to bring this human life and all its endowments to fruition.

The Four Reminders

This human existence with all its freedoms and endowments is
     extremely difficult to attain.
It enables one to accomplish the meaning of one's being.
Having attained such a precious existence,
If one does not accomplish benefit at this time,
How could one achieve this perfect treasure in the future?

The three realms are as impermanent as autumn clouds.
The births and deaths of beings are like a dance performance.
Flashing by like lightning in the sky, the life span of beings
Races swiftly like a waterfall over a steep mountain.

When the time comes for even a king to depart,
Neither his riches nor loved ones, relatives, and friends will follow.
Wherever beings abide, wherever they go,
Karma alone follows them like a shadow.

Overpowered by existence, craving, and ignorance,
All beings—humans, gods, and beings of the three lower realms—
Circle unwittingly in the five realms of existence
Like the spinning of a potter's wheel.

The three realms blaze with the sufferings of old age and sickness,
And there is no protector from the raging flames of death.
Born into cyclic existence, beings dwell continually in ignorance,
Circling like bees trapped in a jar.

*Translated by Jetsün Dechen Paldrön and edited by the Dharmasri
Translation Group, Baltimore, 2001*

Introduction:
Approaching the Gateway

WE TAKE SUCH PRIDE in human life and think of ourselves as the most intelligent, sensible form of existence. Yet with all of our endowments, we still cannot find happiness or peace. Unable to realize our human potential and possibilities, we allow an entire lifetime to slip away—a lifetime that could be of such tremendous benefit to ourselves and others. What is the obstacle to sharing, caring, and having loving-kindness for all sentient beings? Why do fabrications or facades arise as barriers to honest human communication? And why do we live in constant extremes of hope and fear without the common sense to do something about it? We really need to think about this.

In the Buddhist tradition, attaining a human life is said to occur as rarely as a blind turtle who, surfacing in a vast ocean once every hundred years, manages to put his head through a wooden yoke floating in all directions on the surface of the water. A more contemporary analogy is the likelihood that a pea dropped from an airplane will be caught on the head of a pin held by someone on the ground. That is how rare—and therefore how precious—a human birth is said to be. With it we attain a precious opportunity—the opportunity to attain enlightenment, or realization, in this lifetime. This opportunity is the result of aspirations made over the course of innumerable lifetimes. From a

Buddhist point of view, when these aspirations mature and meet with the right conditions and teachers, it is possible for us to enter the path of practice and attain enlightenment. For such rare circumstances to come to fruition, we must understand our relationship to this path.

What Is Enlightenment?

Human beings have such an attraction to complexity. We seem to think that if it's so difficult just to earn the money for a square meal, enlightenment must be very difficult, mysterious, and complicated indeed. It doesn't occur to our commonsense mind to actually see where these teachings are leading. When we enter a path of practice, we have to know where it goes. We have to enter the spiritual path with our eyes wide open. From the ultimate point of view and from the very beginning, we're talking about attaining enlightenment, which is very simply the innate nature of all sentient beings.

Enlightenment is not about becoming something or someone else. It is the recognition of our intrinsic human nature, which is absolute truth. This absolute true nature is called buddha nature. The term *buddha*, from the Sanskrit *tathat* or *tathagata*, means "gone beyond," going beyond an ignorant state to become completely inseparable from absolute truth, which is our genuine ground. This is the essence of Buddhism and the main focus of our understanding and practice.

Enlightenment goes by many names: absolute truth, nirvana, liberation, freedom from suffering, freedom from ignorance, buddha mind, true nature of mind, fundamental ground, *tathagatagarbha, sugatagarbha*, nature of suchness, "as it is," primordial wisdom, emptiness and luminosity, bliss and emptiness, and wisdom and compassion. All of these terms refer to ultimate realization. This is the fruition that brings sentient beings from the state of ignorance to complete freedom. And this is our aspiration as we begin to practice. Never lose touch with this: When the fruition is truly understood, the ground we stand on and the path we walk on must be maintained with the same understanding.

Buddha nature is the heart quality of all sentient beings. It is necessary to recognize this core essence in ourselves as well as in others. Our own basic nature is free from ignorance, grasping, and conceptual judgments. There is no room for illusion or falsity in absolute truth. Because it's inseparable from wisdom and compassion, there is no room for evil, greed, selfishness, ignorance, anger, or attachment. This intrinsic ground of goodness is undeniable. All beings appreciate qualities of goodness, wisdom, compassion, and kindness because this is our fundamental nature. Being aware of this is one thing, however; maintaining that awareness is something else.

The Suffering of Samsara

The first thing the Buddha taught after his enlightenment was the truth of suffering, the cause of which is ignorance. Because of ignorance, we are unable to see the compositeness of our perceptions—all the physical and mental forces that come together to create this seemingly solid world. This leads to grasping and the endless cycle of suffering called samsara. Samsara and all its suffering begin when we get caught up in solidifying external appearances instead of remaining on our fundamental ground.

Contemplation

Ask yourself if it is necessary to make such great issues of the things arising from the compositeness of our senses. We can feel and understand these experiences, but none of them is solid. The moment we say "happiness," for example, that moment has moved on. We may assume that this is the same happiness of a few moments ago, but other than the grasping mind that *thinks* it is so, nothing actually stays the same. We could spend a lifetime fixated on experiences of happiness, anger, ignorance, hatred, or jealousy. To really understand suffering, think about the magnitude and intensity of the suffering caused by grasping.

There are many ways to look at suffering. We've all experienced difficulties, pain, and some amount of tragedy in our lives. We've all lost people who were very dear and close to us. Even now, some of us may be suffering from very difficult diseases or difficult times. Most of us, however, have had comfortable lives untouched by the Buddha's noble truth of suffering. We've seen very little of suffering in its entirety, which is what "the suffering of all sentient beings" actually means.

Because we've seen so little suffering, we have no real aversion to samsara, which still seems like a very nice place to be— attractive, with plenty of room in which to live and indulge ourselves. We never stop to consider that all sentient beings want happiness and freedom from suffering just as much as we do. That kind of selfishness and inability to understand our interdependence is a manifestation of ignorance, which creates samsara.

If you have any attraction or devotion to the path of practice, any sense that it is really helpful and beneficial, you must ask yourself, "How well do I truly understand suffering?" The purpose of these teachings is to help us see the depth of suffering in the world and the cause of that suffering, which is ignorance. Ignorance is the one—if very invisible—cause of unhappiness in this world. It is the one thing that prevents simple awareness and genuine human goodness and kindness from arising without obstructions. In the form of habitual tendencies, it distracts us from our fundamental nature—which nevertheless remains constant and complete, like the luminosity of the sun.

The Three Root Poisons

A mind that cannot remain in the fundamental ground of awareness is continuously shifting and creating judgments of liking, disliking, or neutrality. This path of division is the way the mind works. Why are we so distracted? From morning to night, the body is moving, speech is moving, mind is moving, and that constant movement creates action. How many of these actions of body, speech, and mind are based on sanity, generosity, compassion, and tolerance? And how many are deeply embedded with anger, desire, or ignorance; contaminated with selfishness, laziness, jealousy, and irritation; and distracted by other inner and outer wanderings? When we realize that all of this confusion is built on a foundation of useless concepts, we begin to see why samsara is called "suffering."

A concept is an idea or thought that we use to elaborate on a perception. This wouldn't be a problem, of course, if all these layers of elaboration were about goodness, harmony, and peace. But in the process of elaborating, we constantly create dualities of good and bad, likes and dislikes, and further elaborations. If we like what we perceive, we grasp and elaborate with emotions arising from attachment and desire. If we dislike something, aggression will try to keep it from arising, causing fear and rejection. From liking and disliking, all the 84,000 emotions arise. A third factor, ignorance, is a sluggish state, which is sometimes referred to as neutral. This doesn't mean it's nonjudgmental; neutrality is just too lazy or distracted to judge, and so appearances drag us around wherever they like. These three basic obstacles arise in all sentient beings. They are known as the three root poisons: desire, or attachment; anger, or aggression; and the poison of ignorance, which constantly creates solidity and form. Having succumbed to nonawareness, we use them to solidify our concepts through elaboration.

There's nothing particularly Buddhist or spiritual about seeing these three basic emotions as poisons. Not only do they not bring us any happiness, they are fully capable of destroying our sanity. And as useless as these emotions are, we constantly succumb to them.

Let's say "Christine" is sitting in front of me. How would we elaborate on Christine? I like Christine, I don't know who Christine is, Christine is asking or answering a question—all these concepts make Christine more and more solid. In the beginning it's just "Christine," then it's a specific someone doing something specific. Christine becomes bigger and bigger and more and more real, and soon everyone knows about Christine. A moment ago there was no Christine for us, and now she fills our mind and everything is about the concept "Christine." This is how we solidify concepts through elaboration—again and again.

What is Christine's true nature free from all elaborations? What is it about Christine that we could actually appreciate as it is, without layers of fabrication? When we look beyond useless judgments based on appearances, we become inseparable from the absolute truth of the fundamental ground. On this basic ground of goodness, we can establish and realize the whole Buddhist path. When the mind shifts away from that ground of awareness into interpretations based on the three root poisons, it becomes the fertile ground for the karmic seeds already sown there. Like a fertile field ready to produce plants, all the *tendrels*, or coincidences—both auspicious and inauspicious—come together to produce their samsaric fruition.

A Flower in Space

In essence, ignorance is nothing more than a supposition. Like something invisible, it only *seems* to be there. Gampopa describes ignorance in his *Jewel Ornament of Liberation* as "a flower in space."

Imagine that you and I are sitting together, and I begin describing for you a very beautiful flower that I'm holding—which you may or may not be able to see. I go on and on about the qualities and magnificence of this flower, but the flower is imaginary, a flower in space. You might call this daydreaming, and because you can't see any flower you find it difficult to believe in it. In the same way, ignorance is the assumption that there is a "flower" in space when in fact there is nothing there.

Similarly, the thoughts and feelings that seem so real—my ignorance, my anger, my desires, my actual existence—are like this imaginary flower, and we can be just as obsessed by them. Certainly these emotions have a definite feeling and texture, but there is no real evidence to prove their existence. They are like flowers in space. From that perspective, we spend our entire lives enslaved by invisible thoughts and emotions with no actual existence. And another lifetime goes by—accumulating even more karmic causes that bring more fruition. This cycle of suffering is never exhausted, and we're unable to pull out of it. This is the essence of samsara. We must truly understand that suffering is caused by the ignorance of sentient beings who are unable to see their true nature.

This world is definitely filled with great suffering—birth, sickness, old age, and death, as well as hatred, violence, pain, and other difficulties—but the *intensity* of that suffering is up to us. We are all very accustomed to making things difficult, complicated, and "necessary." Grasping at such intense illusions, we allow formless thoughts to become so real that they completely overpower us and our human sensibility to just *be*—simple human beings, honest and kind.

The Compositeness of Perceptions

How do we create this solid environment and these circumstances we're so involved with? Everything we perceive is the result of our six senses—eyes, ears, nose, mouth, bodily touch, and mind consciousness—working together. As the mind consciousness tries to understand and combine these forces, we begin to react to the different perceptions that arise. But ultimately each formation comes back to a thought.

For example, when consciousness arises from the mind to relate an object of sight through the sense organ of the eyes, these three create the first thought of "Oh, I see." The same thing happens when the ear comes together with a sound and sense consciousness. A single sound can divide the mind into the three kinds of ignorance and create karma. The relationship of the six sense organs, six sense objects, and the six sense consciousnesses brings about a "first thought." This is our opportunity to recognize the true nature of that perception and remain within it—or to shift into judging what we see, in which case it becomes something we like, dislike, or want to ignore, and endless concepts are created.

As long as we are not dead, our bodies and minds—with their sense organs, sense objects, and sense consciousnesses—are constantly moving, which produces the constant perception of activity. Recognizing this, we begin to understand the root cause of the endless churning of emotions and pain. It is only through understanding the compositeness of relative reality that the inner essence—which we call "absolute"—can be truly understood.

From the Buddhist perspective, everything arises from mind: all our perceptions and feelings, as well as the external environment and our relationship to it. Every imaginable difficulty or emotion—happiness, suffering, anger, ignorance, desire, attachment, jealousy, hatred—is nothing but an assumption of mind. From this perspective, everything we try to hold on to is a dream: our good life, bad life, happy or sad life, complicated or simple life, spiritual or samsaric life is just a dream that we spend our lives elaborating. As we move from one perception to the next, grasping makes things solid, solidity brings judgment, and judgment keeps us busy. Grasping, judging, and solidifying appearances is unnecessary entertainment that never allows us to recognize their true nature.

Grasping at a self creates aggression; grasping at other creates attachment—and the more we hold on, the more real they become. We might find ourselves saying, "I'm so angry! How depressing that nobody appreciates how huge my anger is, how badly it needs to be analyzed, demonstrated, and given a history and someone to blame." But what good is all this concreteness we're holding on to—other than our assumption that it protects our ego? We might hold on to anger for an entire lifetime—which doesn't harm anyone but ourselves. Only we experience the real difficulties and disappointments of such a life. Life goes on and no one is any the worse for our anger. The sun continues to shine, the earth and moon continue to revolve, and the sky is still there. So whose loss is it? In a moment of true necessity such as death, it's just another thought labeled "anger"—no different from any other thought and of no benefit to ourselves or anyone else. From this point of view, we might look at our anger and see that it's only somewhat real; we might actually be able to talk and laugh about it.

Looking at the empty nature of all phenomena is like peeling away the trunk of a banana tree. The big trunk of a banana tree looks very solid, but it's just a formation of leaves, one over the other. Peel away all the layers of leaves and there's no tree trunk left. A meditator is able to see samsara in the same way. In essence, none of the appearances and experiences we work with has a complicated nature or solid form. Like the banana tree, they're illusions. It's a question of how seriously we take them. How seriously do we take this moment—and how is this any different from a dream?

Everything arises from within ourselves like the dreams we

dream when we sleep at night. You might experience great fear, for example, if you dream of a ferocious animal coming to eat you up. When you wake up, you see that it is only a dream. No matter what good or bad experiences we have in our dreams, when we wake up we see they were never there.

Discovering Our True Nature

Discovering our absolute true nature is the essence of the practice of Buddhism, which is a nontheistic philosophy. Buddhism is not about saving ourselves or others; it's not about letting go of this or that or achieving this or that. All of these polarities or extremes that begin with an action and end with a result are merely *supports* for absolute truth.

This might seem like a contradiction. How can absolute truth beyond concepts rely on a subject and object—or on theistic notions such as a shrine, sacredness, or a path? Why, instead of just getting down to the core essence, do we talk about six realms with even further categories and details? Why do we now have even more forms and divisions than we had before? The purpose of all the different forms of teaching and learning, practices, *sadhanas*, rituals, and so on is to provide a path to the realization of inner essence, which is absolute truth.

To work with a mind that continuously makes logical excuses and hides behind habitual concepts, we have all the different colors and forms such as shrines and teachers, vows, precepts, and other disciplines and philosophies. When we sit in the shrine room, which we call a sacred place, facing representations of the buddhas, bodhisattvas, and teachers, or directly in front of a teacher, we're building in certain restrictions. We create these forms and environments in the hope that—at least in the moment—we can be more honest and have more determination and openness than we do in our daily life with its chaos, confusion, and habitual patterns. In this way, one step at a time, we can develop the real courage of mind to do things differently. This is how we move toward enlightenment.

Enlightenment is recognizing the true nature of every appearance—sound, sight, smell, form, taste, touch, thought, or feeling—that arises. It is recognizing that this display of perceptions is an illusion. It is empty, empty in the sense that nothing is solid. We can view every experience—everything we do, relate to, or try to make sense of—as a dream. The Buddhist path is simply a way of working with these dreams. There is nothing mysterious about working with the dreamlike, or empty, nature of things.

Working with Relative Reality

When we talk about the illusory nature of things, we are not criticizing the relative reality of our perceptions, and we're not trying to stop *liking* all the things that we see, hear, and so on. We are trying to see their compositeness and not make them more "real" than necessary. Buddhist practice is a way to understand that. When we walk out the door after meditation, all our perceptions and emotions will seem real. From them, we create our worlds—your world, my world—and from that come selfishness, ego-grasping, and all the complexity of conditioned existence. Buddhist practice is a way to understand that as long as our sense perceptions function, we can work with the notion that they are not all that real.

We are not trying to destroy what is there; we're trying to develop an openness of mind. An open mind is not so worried about things. There is less *worriedness* about making things more real than necessary—and less worriedness about needing to make them unreal. Otherwise, we could spend a lifetime trying to renounce attachment to our world—which is one path of practice, and sometimes it's helpful. As monastics, we might renounce family, property, land, and money and make lists of the things that we're attached to. But a simpler way to get to the root of things is to simply work with our minds.

If we could recognize the empty nature of just *one* thought, we would understand the inherent emptiness of all thoughts. It's not necessary to work through the solidity of every concept to reach the state of exhaustion: we don't have to exhaust all ignorance, attachment, desire, ignorance, hatred, and jealousy. We need only recognize that the nature of mind is inherently and truly free from grasping. This alone brings freedom from illusions. Anything else provides fertile ground for the production of karma: when mind shifts from awareness to nonawareness, limitless karmic seeds grow in that ground and come to fruition, and the cycle of suffering continues.

These Instructions Are Being Given to You

As Buddhist practitioners, we're following the example of Shakyamuni Buddha. When the Buddha first attained enlightenment, the first thing he taught was the nature of absolute truth, the fundamental true nature of mind. But no one understood him. The Buddha then taught the first noble truth of suffering. Now, you might think that just because that ignorant group didn't get it 2,500 years ago, we have to deal with all these rituals and listen to 84,000 tenet teachings and commentaries, and so on. These instructions, however, are being given to you.

If Shakyamuni Buddha were sitting in front of you presenting the absolute true nature of mind, would you be able to understand it and put it into practice—even today, with all your potential and access to Buddhist teachings? And if I were to tell you that, because the nature of mind is emptiness and luminosity, all you need to do is let go of all grasping—that's all that Buddhism is about—could you do it? There's a difference between understanding this view and being able to hold it and put it into practice. For this, we must transcend habitual patterns of body, speech, and mind.

The Challenge of Habitual Patterns

Although intrinsic basic goodness is within all of us, we still come face to face with tremendous challenges known as habitual patterns. Our enthusiasm and awareness may be challenged by emotional afflictions such as ignorance, desire, hatred, jealousy, or anger.

More often than not, we succumb to these distractions. Most of us are so preoccupied with our habitual patterns that we've lost the simplicity of absolute truth, which is no longer reflected in the actions of our body, speech, and mind. Failing to maintain our awareness of fundamental truth we come to depend on the falsity of appearances, or false views. We then base all our judgments on what is *apparent* rather than true. If anger arises, for example, rather than looking into the depth of another person's heart, we judge the sounds and actions we perceive—which gives rise to endless elaborations. We are then unable to realize our genuine nature. We could say that, ultimately, enlightenment is the exhaustion of all such concepts.

Habitual patterns provide us with a ground of familiarity. It's the familiar way we've lived this life and innumerable other lives; the familiar way we solidify every feeling, perception, thought, and action. It's the familiar way we make things real—elaborating, judging, and expanding—and then cater to that reality and try to survive in it. We may not like our anger, for example, but if anger is our habitual ground it's more familiar than tolerance. And in spite of our aspirations, we're unable to let go of anger and turn to tolerance. We are constantly faced with the challenge of breaking through what have become very set patterns of thinking, speaking, and living.

We Don't Need to Begin by Changing the World

Much has already been written about spiritual practice. Everyone understands spiritual materialism and agrees that it is the quality, not the quantity, of practice that's important. And in spite of all the practices and philosophies, we do understand that it's the *mind* that needs to be trained and that if we are on the path of meditation, we do need to develop compassion and kindness. But we don't need to begin by changing the world or transforming all ignorance into wisdom. First of all, when we enter the profound path and practice of meditation, compassion toward sentient beings is a given; their benefit is inherent in our meditation and practice. Before we think about generating compassion for the suffering and ignorance of all beings, we must first learn to see through our own illusions.

Seeing our experience as illusion is not a way of destroying relative reality. It's a way of working with its absolute essence, which is our own true nature. Otherwise we end up creating endless complexities and spend lifetimes trying to make things solid when they're not. From this seeming solidity arises the constant flickering of "mine and yours," and other emotions such as searching, wanting, and anxiety. Above all, there's the intensity of ignorance: wanting happiness, we're unable to create the cause of happiness; wanting to walk in one direction, we walk the opposite way—hoping against hope that something will change. How many of us end up doing this very thing?

Taking Control of Your Life

Because ignorance doesn't allow our human sensibilities to develop or express themselves fully or properly, it creates a prison-like situation. In this conditioned world of samsara, why can we not express our real truth and potential completely? It's because we're unable to control our bodies, our speech, or our minds. Understanding this, we begin to see what the suffering of samsara is really about.

Since you have this precious human life, you must have some control over it. If you decide, for example, that you'd really like not to harm others physically, it should be possible not to do so. There should be no obstacle to physically expressing flexibility and kindness. And there should be no real obstacle to kindness arising in your speech. You should be able to use your speech properly, with discipline, in a way that truly benefits others. And, if you're generating thoughts in your mind, you need to have some control over your mind.

Having control over your body, speech, and mind is like being a skillful rider. You can go where you want to go; the horse goes in the direction that *you* want to go in. An unskilled rider trying to ride a wild horse eventually ends up wherever the horse wants to go. In the same way, you may find your body going in one direction, your speech in another—and the rest of your sensibilities not waking up until quite a bit later, if then. The whole framework of the Buddhist path—the various levels and practices and forms for sitting, standing, thinking, and behaving—is a support for learning to work with our mental concepts and developing the ability to maintain awareness. And from a Buddhist point of view, training the mind through meditation is essential.

Training the Mind through Meditation
The path of meditation works with the root, which is mind. Chasing after everything else will keep you busy, but no real inner change or transformation will arise from your spiritual practice. It's like the popular game show I saw on German TV: lots of colorful balls keep popping up from a hole, and players with sticks in their hands try to hit the balls as soon as they arise. The more balls you hit, the more points you win. Our meditation is sometimes

like that: we sit and wait for our so-called obstacles—attachment, desire, hatred, jealousy—to pop up. Then, holding our spiritual philosophies in our hands, we try to hit them as soon as they arise. This keeps us very busy and we have a sense of getting things done. But other than boosting our ego, we cannot really say we're meditating—nor will this bring the freedom from ignorance that we seek. Creating a spiritual illusion is no better than creating any other illusion.

The main point of meditation practice, the essence of Dharma itself, is to be completely honest and to work with that honesty in a simple way. To understand the practice of meditation is to understand *simplicity*. The basic foundation of the teachings lies in how very simple and ordinary—and yet how profound—things can be. No meditator can afford to get caught up in things that aren't all that necessary. We really need to understand this: instead of creating great seriousness and grave issues, we need to lighten up and open ourselves up to our true nature.

Meditation enables us to see the seed of enlightenment in every emotion or thought so that any concept can bring awareness of our fundamental ground. When the mind rests in awareness, there is no ground for the creation of karma, and nothing causes the mind to shift into unawareness or solidify concepts. The ground and path of our practice are completely based on the exhaustion of ignorance and false views. Any trace of conceptualizing the ground or path is a gap between our path and fruition. If the aim of our meditation is to exhaust all concepts, then the view and path must be free from concepts as well. Maintaining a conceptual attitude in meditation won't lead to a nonconceptual state, will it? If we want sweet fruit, we have to plant a sweet seed. Or, as Tibetans say: if you want to go north, you have to walk north; you can't get to the north by walking south. Of course, this example is completely outdated, since we all know the world is round; nevertheless, if we want freedom from samsara, we need to go in that direction. From a Buddhist perspective, enlightenment is freedom from concepts and elaboration. To see the emptiness of concepts and elaboration is why we meditate.

Crossing Over: The Four Thoughts That Transform the Mind

The path of practice leads us out of ignorance and grasping and brings us to the state called nirvana, or enlightenment. This is referred to as "crossing over"—crossing over to realize absolute truth, which completely removes every stain of ignorance that obscures the mind. In this way, the true nature of things can be understood. One of the best supports for this path is the contemplation of the Four Thoughts That Transform the Mind.

Contemplation is another simple antidote for the solid concepts we're so attached to. Using the theory "like cures like," we can use a concept to cure a concept. We can use a positive thought to transform a negative thought. By transforming negative concepts into positive concepts, we enter into a deeper understanding of the true essence or meaning. This is what the hinayana and mahayana practice paths are about. Mind then becomes mature enough to understand transcendence, which is what the vajrayana teachings are about.

First, *contemplating the preciousness of human existence* brings a genuine appreciation of our human body, mind, and potential. With exertion, we can actually create the cause for genuine happiness and benefit for others.

Contemplating impermanence brings a sense of urgency about not wasting that potential and exerting more effort. *Contemplating the suffering of the six realms* enables us not to conceptualize selflessness and exertion. Whether we read about it or actually experience it, the pain of sentient beings should turn our minds toward exertion and effort. In that way, we become free from the ignorance that creates confusion and unnecessary suffering.

Contemplating both impermanence and suffering brings a strong motivation to create the fundamental ground of good karma. With a ground of good, positive actions, we can attain happiness and the cause of happiness for ourselves and others. Otherwise there would be no reason to contemplate such things.

Contemplating karma develops awareness and helps us to understand the intricacies of a mind that continually slips back into habitual patterns. We may aspire to selflessness and freedom from habitual conceptualizing, but just talking about them is not enough if we lack the awareness to put these things into practice. Contemplating karma, we realize the need for the support of constant mindfulness and awareness. We also understand the importance of aspiring to compassion and freedom from suffering for all sentient beings. If our compassion is truly genuine, there won't be any lack of awareness; if there *is* a lack of awareness, we need to strengthen our aspiration and put it into action.

Contemplating karma challenges us to see whether awareness has been truly planted and strengthened in our mind as a result of contemplating the other three reminders. Seeing the diversity of suffering that karma creates, we want all sentient beings to be free from suffering. It's not just about us saving ourselves or escaping from samsara. It's about the exertion we put into bringing all of our human endowments to fruition.

The teachings on suffering and karma are not meant to lead to paralyzing fear or a solidification of the realms and their sufferings. Instead, they enable us to create positive circumstances from adverse circumstances. Because our effort is nonconceptual, we can put that effort into the right path, the path of genuine compassion. Compassion arises for all sentient beings, who, through a single moment of ignorance, are stuck in painful creations that they don't want but continue to create.

Contemplating the Four Reminders and bringing them to the path brings an understanding of the path and the practices.

Otherwise, if we're simply dabbling in Buddhism, we might get stuck at those points that we like or dislike, conceptualizing them and making them solid. Then history would repeat itself: mind would come up with very spiritual reasons that it shouldn't let go of grasping; we would revert to habitual actions, and our aspiration to benefit beings would never be accomplished.

This contemplation doesn't need to be sequential or even particularly Buddhist. The Four Reminders bring the mind back again and again to the ground of awareness, which becomes stronger. When habitual patterns strike, awareness is there, and we can go on our way, maintaining even greater awareness. We will contemplate the Four Reminders in the following chapters, beginning with the preciousness of human existence.

First Thought: The Preciousness of a Human Birth

This human existence with all its freedoms and
endowments is extremely difficult to attain.
It enables one to accomplish the meaning of one's being.
Having attained such a precious existence,
If one does not accomplish benefit at this time,
How could one achieve this perfect treasure in the future?

Each human life is completely endowed with the potential for absolute enlightenment. Each of our lives could be an enormous blessing to ourselves and others. At the very least, each of us could achieve a harmonious and peaceful life and bring a seed of happiness into others' lives.

When we talk about benefiting others, we must begin by recognizing our inherent buddha nature—which could simply be called human nature, as they both refer to the fundamental ground of our being. This is a ground of goodness that is not contaminated with ignorance. Completely understanding this ground of genuine goodness would give us irreversible confidence in it.

Irreversible Confidence

IRREVERSIBLE CONFIDENCE comes from recognizing and being sure of the presence of our fundamental ground. With growing confidence, we are no longer distracted by laziness, disappointments, sadness, enthusiasm, and so on. We no longer have to succumb to ignorance—or aggression, attachment, selfishness, or habitual tendencies such as irritation, jealousy, or aggravation. Recognizing our core essence of enlightenment, we appreciate the preciousness of our existence.

When we underestimate our human existence, tendencies such as laziness arise. With laziness, we remain "as we were," distracted and stuck in habitual patterns. We could say that *any* tendency to distraction impedes the arising of buddha nature—again, due to not appreciating the preciousness of each moment. To conquer these distractions, contemplate the preciousness of human existence.

Appreciating one's life generates a courageous heart and a courageous mind. Knowing that we could become completely free and lead others to freedom from endless and intolerable suffering, we can live with a sense of urgency and complete awareness—

which brings confidence and joy and even greater appreciation of our life and potential. Then we can encounter moments of depression or disappointment without succumbing to hopes and fears based on emotions, concepts, or habitual tendencies. And we can conquer discursive thoughts of ordinariness, weakness, or inadequacy—recognizing them as mere tricks of the mind.

Of course, mind will put up a fierce fight when it comes to ignorance and habitual patterns. In its struggle to preserve its identity and territory, it will come up with all sorts of *nonappreciation* of our fundamental true nature and highlight all our negative characteristics and tendencies. One way that ignorance gains a victory over our wisdom mind is by highlighting our negative tendencies through self-criticism.

With all our study and practice, we may still find it difficult to encourage ourselves on the path. Instead we criticize ourselves and feel inadequate or disappointed in our lack of awareness, our gender bias, or our inability to keep vows and precepts. When we criticize ourselves, ignorance demonstrates its tendencies. We may assume that by being self-critical we're actually doing something good. Of course, it is important to recognize faults and overcome negative tendencies, but we often sink into the ignorance of criticizing ourselves without seeing our positive qualities. If we look carefully, we will see there are far more positive qualities than negative tendencies.

Because of our inherent buddha nature, our positive qualities —the very ground from which everything arises—are stronger and more numerous than our negativities. But because of habitual mind, we focus on the bleakness of our ignorance and negative qualities. We don't see ourselves as genuinely qualified and worthy vessels for the teachings. Eventually this negativity becomes so strong that it completely covers up anything bright, luminous, and genuinely good arising from our inherently pure nature. The antidote to this pessimism and self-criticism is to understand the preciousness of human existence. It's essential to strengthen the mind in this way.

Contemplation

In meditation, watch for signs of blaming: blaming yourself for not being a better practitioner, for allowing the mind to slip into unawareness, and so on. Watch out for the habit of highlighting negative tendencies or inabilities. This will prevent you from generating the courage necessary to put your body, speech, and mind fully on the path of practice.

2

The Eighteen Qualities of a Precious Human Existence

A PRECIOUS HUMAN LIFE is endowed with eighteen qualities. So that we may better understand them, they are divided into eight freedoms and ten endowments. The term for
qualities is loosely translated from the Tibetan *dalwa jorwa* (*dal ba
'byor ba*). *Dalwa* usually signifies "freedom," and *jorwa*—literally
"riches," "wealth," or "endowment"—here refers to the intrinsic
richness or essence of mind. The great treasure master Terdag
Lingpa also explains *dal* as the essence of "resting:" we are "free
from being separated from resting in the essence of mind."

Separation occurs in the mind when the conceptual thoughts
that arise separate us from our ground of intrinsic awareness. We
then succumb to appearances, which leads to fabrication and the
creation of samsara. The eight freedoms allow us to remain in a
state of nonseparation from the ground of awareness. Because we
are constantly exposed to various distractions, this is difficult to
do. To remain in a completely uncontrived state is the actual
meaning of *shamatha* meditation, or "calm abiding." So the endowments embody freedom, the fundamental essence of mind;
and the ten endowments and eight freedoms make up the eight-

een qualities, because of which a human life is said to be precious. The reason for contemplating these eighteen qualities is to recognize our own goodness and potential. This can bring happiness to ourselves and others.

⊙ *Contemplation*

Having understood your core essence of enlightenment, you can rely on the process of analysis if you then revert back to habitual tendencies. Ask yourself, "How do these emotions arise? What is their nature? Are they useful or not? Can they be proven?" Study the teachings and apply them in meditation so that understanding and appreciation come about.

We cannot understand and cultivate our human qualities properly by comparing ourselves or competing with others. Instead we must look at exactly how to put these qualities into practice. This is like having an abundance of good food and wanting to cook something to eat. Let's say we have eighteen main ingredients laid out on the table in front of us. We could prostrate to our ingredients and recite their names faithfully; we could hang up their pictures and make daily supplications to them—and we would die of hunger! It's the same with Dharma. No matter how loyal and devoted we are, no matter how much we supplicate and say, "I love you," until we truly put it into practice, the Dharma won't ripen within us. The point is to bring the eighteen qualities to fruition.

3

The Eight Freedoms

T HE EIGHT FREEDOMS are counted among the eighteen qualities because they strengthen our fundamental pure nature and are necessary to bring the teachings on absolute truth to fruition.

THE FIRST THREE FREEDOMS refer to freedom from birth in the three lower realms: the hell, hungry ghost, and animal realms. (We will talk about the six realms individually in part 3.) The extreme conditions and suffering of the lower realms prevent us from becoming aware of our intrinsic nature and potential to benefit ourselves and others. Because our awareness is so completely on the immediate experience of suffering, the lower realms are improbable conditions in which to generate enlightened mind.

THE FOURTH FREEDOM is freedom from birth in a barbarous place. This is sometimes mistakenly thought of as a tribal place, but it actually refers to a country without any understanding of the ten virtuous and unvirtuous actions. In a barbaric place, there is no understanding of genuine selflessness and the need to refrain from selfish activities. There is no understanding of the need for compassion and no awareness of the human responsibility to do the right thing. We are solely preoccupied with our own survival—feeding ourselves, our self-identity, and so on. And we're not even faintly aware of the happiness of others. Harming others seems acceptable. There are no favorable conditions for generating awareness or bodhichitta, and therefore we're completely unaware of the need to break free from such patterns. This condition is referred to as a barbarous place. It doesn't mean that beings in these realms have an inferior nature; it simply refers to the difficulty of remaining in an uncontrived state when surrounded by extremely distracting circumstances. Freedom from birth in such a place is also something that you and I have attained.

THE FIFTH FREEDOM is not being born in the god (*deva*) realm, which is the fruition of virtuous actions and merit that are contaminated with selfishness. This is a pleasurable life free from immediate pain and suffering—but still not free from cyclic existence. The intense pleasures of the god realm bring no awareness of the importance of letting go of ignorance or unvirtuous activities. In certain god realms, we simply have a sense of "Oh, I've been born in the deva realm." Such a life is like a long, comfortable sleep.

The end result, however, is the exhaustion of the good karma that brought us there. When we have exhausted our good karma, negative karmas catch up with us and we are born into one of the other realms. For this reason, birth in the god realm is said to be even worse than birth in the three lower realms. With all their pain and suffering, the lower realms actually exhaust our negative karma. In the god realm it is temporarily suppressed, which only makes it last longer—meanwhile, all the good karma we've accumulated is being completely exhausted. And even without the suffering of the lower realms, we are still unable to practice or realize our intrinsic nature. Intense preoccupation with desire and attachment is so thick that—just as with extreme suffering—we never meet with the circumstances leading to awareness. Because we are unable to generate enlightened mind, birth in the god realm is as unfavorable as birth in the lower realms. Since you have not been born in these realms, you are free from these conditions.

THE SIXTH FREEDOM is freedom from wrong view. We may indeed be born in a place where we meet with the Dharma and be aware of the fundamental goodness of human nature, yet we don't cultivate these valuable qualities. We have no faith in cause and effect and no genuine devotion to the qualities of the Three Jewels. This is wrong view, which is more intense than simply lacking awareness. With wrong view, we actually cause harm to ourselves and others. This occurs because we just don't see the whole meaning and point of generating goodness, compassion, or selflessness, and so we continue to base our actions in selfishness and unkindness. We need to understand that we do know right from wrong. This is a mind that is sane, a mind that knows that good actions bring happiness and negative actions create suffering. Nevertheless, we choose to continue negative activities, ignoring cause and effect and the harm we inflict.

Now, it's important not to misunderstand wrong view or to be too tough on yourself. None of us has complete confidence in cause and effect at this point, and it's quite fair to say we all have wrong view to some extent. You needn't lose sleep at night thinking, "I'm the anti-Buddhist, the one with no confidence in cause and effect." Please don't be too hard on yourself.

Freedom from wrong view means that we understand the importance of generating awareness and abandoning unvirtuous activities. As long as we recognize the harmfulness and negativity of anger, desire, ignorance, jealousy, and hatred, and the need to abandon these, we do not hold a wrong view. (We will talk more about freedom from wrong view as a fruition of refuge in part 5.)

THE SEVENTH FREEDOM is not being born in a place without the presence of a buddha. This could be a place where the buddhas have not come to teach. If we never met the Dharma, having a human birth with all its endowments wouldn't matter. We wouldn't have any opportunity to learn, practice, or find the path to liberation. Or, we might be born in a time and place with a buddha—we might even live next door to a Buddhist center—but, because of our karmic conditions, we have no idea that a being called Buddha or the path of meditation exists in this world. For us it is as if the Buddha had never come and taught. Contemplate the fact that you're not suffering from this obstruction. You've been born in a time when the Buddha has come, in a place where the Buddha has taught.

THE EIGHTH FREEDOM is not being born deaf and dumb. This needs to be understood properly. The Tibetan term *kukpa* (*lkug pa*) is translated as "deaf and mute." A person who is deaf and mute from birth has never had the opportunity to hear the Dharma. Without this opportunity, it's very difficult for such a person to put effort into the path of practice. Due to good karma, however, he or she may have a natural ability to generate kindness, compassion, and actions that show basic goodness. We may know such a person, and in his or her basic nature we may find goodness and the ability to know right from wrong. Such a precious human existence is qualified to attain absolute realization within one lifetime. So this is by no means a criticism of anyone; it's a way of acknowledging how easy it is for us.

We are actually talking about those who have no understanding of what to accept and reject, no ability to abandon negative tendencies and cultivate the good. Whatever the circumstantial reasons, such people will have difficulty generating enlightened mind, for the simple reason that they cannot distinguish between good and bad actions. If you understand the difference between good and bad and we know what to abandon and cultivate—even if we are impaired or disabled—you are not in this category.

Awareness of the conditions that we are *not* suffering from should bring an understanding of all the fortunate circumstances we do have. The reason for contemplating the eighteen qualities is to recognize our own goodness and potential, which can bring happiness to ourselves and others. So if you see a fault in yourself, the wisest thing to do is to change it. If you see that you lack confidence in karma, try harder to understand cause and effect; don't mope about or criticize yourself for not having enough confidence. From today onward, bring more awareness to cause and effect and get to work on it. That's a more positive way of looking at things. What's being asked of us is not that we become good Buddhists but that we develop a genuine awareness of exactly what we're doing with our lives.

> There is no greater example of ignorance than a
>   meditator who,
> Having contemplated the rarity of all these endowments,
> Still does not understand the value of this life
> And continues to waste it.*

Waiting for enlightenment will not bring about enlightenment. The conditions leading to enlightenment must be acted upon. If we know this to be so, and yet the tendency to wait and wait continues in meditation, there's a very big gap between aspi-

---

* From the *Bodhicharyavatara,* by Shantideva. Translated by the author from Tibetan.

ration and practice. The intention of anyone on the path of practice is to cross over from ignorance to pristine wisdom. This will happen only when our body, speech, and mind are completely grounded in letting go. We must be willing to let go of laziness, aggression, ignorance, desire, attachment and grasping, jealousy, and hatred. Reflecting on all the positive conditions with which we're endowed will make it possible to let go of these habitual tendencies.

The eight freedoms alone provide enough inspiration, guidance, and path to bring the aspiration for selfless compassion to fruition. Don't they? At this point, other than our own unwillingness to let go of self-grasping, we're completely endowed with favorable inner and outer conditions. Recognizing the rarity of these qualities, we are free from ignorance, the cause of suffering. As practitioners on the path of meditation, it is essential for us to remain in this understanding of the preciousness of human existence. To support that, contemplate the eight freedoms.

Contemplation

Go through the eight freedoms one by one. Reflect on the various distractions and kinds of pain they describe, and how very few and small your own problems are by comparison. See that your problems—which you often create yourself—have solutions. In this way reflect on the eight freedoms with a true sense of what a great opportunity you have in the preciousness of this moment and this existence.

4

The Ten Endowments

THE TEN ENDOWMENTS are divided into five self-endowments and five circumstantial endowments. Together with the eight freedoms, they constitute the eighteen qualities of a precious human existence. The eight freedoms and five self-endowments are similar in that each of them discusses the negative conditions leading to nonfreedom and the opposite qualities giving rise to freedom. Look to see if these qualities are present within you—and if they are, know how truly fortunate your circumstances are.

The Five Self-Endowments

THE FIRST SELF-ENDOWMENT is having a human body and a mind that is capable of generating compassion and wisdom. Although a human birth is still within the realms of samsara, it is a valuable vessel. Without this human body, it wouldn't be possible to be a container for absolute truth. This body and mind are able to realize the essence of enlightenment and to take that essence into action for the benefit of all sentient beings. It is important to appreciate the preciousness of this existence.

THE SECOND SELF-ENDOWMENT is that our human body has been born in a "central land." This is a land where the buddhas, bodhisattvas, and teachers have taught, where Dharma continues to be taught and practiced, and where the wheel of Dharma continues to be turned. Traditionally, a "central land" refers to Bodhgaya, the actual place where the Buddha attained enlightenment and first taught. In the Buddhist teachings, however, we need to be aware of all the different meanings of each word. The word *Bodhgaya*, for example, comes from the Sanskrit word *bodhi*, which literally means "awakening." Another name for Bodhgaya is Vajrasana, which can mean the "land of vajra," or "vajra mind," which is none other than buddha mind. So being born in a central land could mean a situation or place where we are presented with the view of vajra mind, a place where we can recognize our inherent buddha nature and take it to complete realization. We have been born in such a place.

THE THIRD SELF-ENDOWMENT is that we're born with our six senses intact. Our eyes can see, our ears can hear, and so forth; and our mind consciousness has the ability to discern right from wrong. Therefore we are able to know what to abandon and what to cultivate. This is the wisdom of discernment. Having all of our senses intact, we can remain in the ground of awareness with all of our perceptions, which is a precious quality.

THE FOURTH SELF-ENDOWMENT is that we're born with the right view. We are not holding the wrong view described earlier. Right view also refers to livelihood. A livelihood that is congruent with the view does not create the ground for any negative karma. Any occupation, job, or responsibility that leads to the creation of negative karma is in complete contradiction to the aspiration of selflessness, generosity, buddha mind, and benefiting sentient beings. Our livelihood should be based on the ground of accumulating positive cause and effect, and its activities should lead to the achievement of our aspirations. Right activity cannot arise from a foundation of wrong livelihood.

The term *livelihood* also has a wide range of interpretations. It's not only our job; it is any responsibility we take on that leads to some action or result. Our responsibility could lead to a negative action, such as a power struggle, jealousy, disparaging comments, or criticism. It might create turmoil in the minds of practitioners. It could manifest as difficulties with one who is in a position of authority, or difficulties among teachers or meditation instructors. Our intentions might be expressed with hardness, in words that cut or injure the mind of another—which is like actually killing that person. A physical killing could have less impact than killing someone's mind and destroying their ground of goodness. It is extremely important to realize how quickly we can create circumstances that can pull other people from their path or disrupt their progress in understanding the Dharma. A livelihood that does not inflict harm—intentionally or unintentionally—on sentient beings is congruent with the view of absolute truth.

THE FIFTH SELF-ENDOWMENT is the quality of devotion, or irreversible confidence. With devotion, we have confidence in our basic true nature and path of practice. We are confident that we can walk on the path and generate selfless compassion for sentient beings. Terdag Lingpa emphasizes that irreversible confidence should be understood as a willingness to be tamed, to go through transformation, and to transcend. This willingness brings the confidence to understand the value of the view—at which point taming, transformation, and transcendence can take place. We could say that taming is related to the hinayana path of practice, transformation is related to the mahayana path, and transcendence is related to the vajrayana path. All three lead to training the mind.

Understanding the value of view means recognizing how grasping leads to the notion of a self, an "I," and seeing how stubbornly we hold on to the belief in a self—and how silly this stubbornness is. Self-grasping is based on fear and the need to preserve and protect our identity. Taming, transformation, and transcendence are connected with letting go of the stubbornness. Reflecting on ignorance and its cause, we can tame, transform, and transcend ignorance, which leads to the dissolution of rigid, self-grasping mind. The fundamental ground can then arise unimpeded.

These are the five self-endowments. Upon reflection we can see they are inherent in us. The only obstacle to their full manifestation is hesitation arising from ignorance. Ignorance can manifest as unawareness, as inner distractions such as depression or disappointment, or as the outer distractions of the senses. Recognizing the preciousness of our endowments, we should exert effort so they reach their full potential.

The Five Circumstantial Endowments

The five circumstantial endowments are five circumstances that permit us to fully utilize all eight freedoms and five self-endowments.

THE FIRST CIRCUMSTANTIAL ENDOWMENT is that the Buddha has come into this world. Throughout the ages, or *kalpas*, there are various ages in which no buddhas are born—or they are born but do not attain enlightenment or do not teach. These are known as dark ages, dark kalpas. When we speak of the history of civilization and the ages of the world, we speak in terms of kalpas. A kalpa lasts for thousands of years and is made up of four stages. First it originates and establishes its existence; second, this existence actually continues. Then comes a gradual disintegration or destruction of that kalpa. Finally, there is the complete extinction or exhaustion of the kalpa. These are the four phases that a world system—and our own experience—goes through.

Within a kalpa, countless buddhas—or no buddhas—may arise, depending on our karmic creations. The same mind that creates the karmic causes and conditions of the six realms has the absolute ability to create kalpas with and without buddhas. If we meet someone on the road who has never heard of the Buddha, for that person this is a dark age. He or she was born in a kalpa with no Buddha, no teachings of Buddha, and no understanding of the wheel of Dharma. There are also kalpas in which buddhas manifest but don't teach. This is also in accord with the conditions of the time. Our circumstances are different: we are endowed with the Buddha and his teachings. Shakyamuni Buddha, who lived 2,500 years ago, turned the wheel of Dharma not just once but several times within our time period. Although he passed into nirvana, the teachings are maintained through an unbroken lineage of Sangha.

In *The Words of My Perfect Teacher*, Patrul Rinpoche explains the formation and meaning of kalpas and the constant arising of world systems. Out of ignorance, we tend to relate only to our personal experience: what my eyes see, ears hear, nose smells, mouth tastes, body feels, and mind thinks. These sense perceptions confirm our ego. We tend to think that everything revolves around our sense perceptions and understanding—and anything beyond them cannot exist, which is a fairly arrogant way of looking at things. So world systems must be appreciated in their entirety.

A simple way to begin is to see the difference between my view of the world and yours. My perceptions and yours are different. The world may look like one big ball, one system that we call the cosmos, but even in that oneness there are different perceptions. There may be the same quality of space, but the perceptions within that space differ. This is because of the way karma is created: every cause has different results. Three individuals will plant three different seeds with three different results. Likewise, a variety of causes with a common ground will generally have a similar fruition. For example, every form of anger creates some kind of pain. But three individuals may have different intentions, different reasons to be angry. Different causes and conditions create different interpretations of anger, resulting in a more or less intense fruition. The difference in fruition is due to differences in our perceptual abilities to create and interpret those creations.

For this reason, there can be sentient beings in this world system who never hear a word of the Buddha's teachings. Such people are born into the same outer circumstances and world system as you are, but in a place and time with no buddha. To think that everyone is in the same big bubble, to think that "my" experience is the same for all sentient beings, is not logical. Of all the billions of sentient beings, how many are actually born in a world system where they experience the Buddha? In this same world system, how many buddhas—due to circumstances of karma—do not teach? We could find ourselves in a world where the Buddha didn't teach, or where the Buddha and his teachings never arrived at all. We could simply never meet with the teachings, or we could meet with them and not connect.

A buddha is a genuinely enlightened being who manifests to benefit sentient beings. In this world system it is said that 1,022 buddhas will be born. Not all buddhas will arise in the same form, dress in the same uniform, teach or sit in the same way, or speak the same language. To expect that they would is to solidify the notion of what an enlightened buddha is. Buddhas arise in the forms that will best benefit sentient beings. Some, like Shakyamuni Buddha, are born to perform innumerable activities. Many manifest through compassion but we never encounter or recognize them as buddhas. There are buddhas who never go through the process of turning the wheel or teaching the Dharma. We have been born in a time when a buddha was born, attained enlightenment, and taught the Dharma—which brings us to the second circumstantial endowment.

The second circumstantial endowment is the Buddha's teachings. If the Buddha had never taught, we'd never be able to meet with or understand the Dharma. We are fortunate not to be in such a situation; we have the opportunity to connect with the teachings and instructions that develop the ground of enlightenment. We are endowed with what is known as "Dharma resting without degeneration": the Dharma still exists and is still being practiced; the purity of the view remains.

The third circumstantial endowment is the good fortune to have been born at a time when the Dharma—with all the goodness and genuineness of the teachings—is still being taught. If we were to be born in a time much later than this, when all the buddhas, bodhisattvas, and great masters had already come and gone, we would live in a degenerate age. In a degenerate age, the strength and power of a world system and the preciousness of its qualities begin to decline. The Dharma becomes weaker and may not be properly practiced. The teachings may be misinterpreted or misunderstood, and misguidance may be given. Our circumstances again are different.

A degenerate age occurs when emphasis is placed on the interpretation of the view rather than the true view itself. It occurs when we misuse or misunderstand the view, taking only what makes sense to us or can be practiced by an ignorant mind. Ignorance contaminates the view by measuring and weighing and allowing hesitation, stubbornness, and ego-grasping to occur. We contaminate the view to make it sound good, feel good, or suit selfish ends. Interpreting the view to suit our own needs and demands, we then present it to others in the same degenerate way. This is known as the full manifestation of the degenerate age. It is rare to be born in circumstances where this hasn't happened, where with right effort we can still meet with the pure Dharma whose meaning has not been interpreted. This is the essential third circumstantial endowment. Recognizing how rare this is, we should exert effort. Do not misuse this opportunity or let it go by.

THE FOURTH CIRCUMSTANTIAL ENDOWMENT is that there are living examples of the Dharma and the practices. The view has been completely preserved, and we are able to encounter the pure view and connect with a Sangha that practices it completely. In the absence of the Buddha, to have living examples with whom we can connect is a rare endowment. In degenerate times there may be Dharma in theory, but living examples are rare. We're nearing a time when our living examples are becoming fewer in number—and there may be some sense of hurrying before we run out of this endowment. But at this point we are still endowed with living masters, living examples, on the path of practice.

THE FIFTH CIRCUMSTANTIAL ENDOWMENT, which is the most important of all, is the genuine kindness in the heart of the teacher. Anyone who teaches the Dharma must have compassion for others. Otherwise, no matter how much effort a teacher exerts, it's likely that the Dharma will be misinterpreted and that students will not be directed to the correct view. So it is essential to be born in a time when teachers have selfless compassion in their hearts. It is said that compassion in the hearts of the students signifies compassion in the hearts of those responsible for teaching the Dharma. Gathering and maintaining favorable circumstances plants the seed of Dharma in the minds of practitioners. Any teacher of Dharma must also have developed awareness and be able to be completely selfless at all times.

It is said that the exact time when the Dharma will fall apart, when the genuine pure Dharma will no longer be taught, will come when Dharma teachers no longer have genuine compassion toward sentient beings. When fabricated compassion or lack of compassion is reflected in the mind or conduct of a teacher and a teacher's priority is self-gain, then the degenerate age is manifest in all its glory. In our time, we are fortunate to have met teachers with genuine compassion who do not teach for personal gain. This is our circumstantial endowment.

Together with our primordially pure nature, these are the inherent circumstances that bring our mind and body to perfect liberation. To realize how difficult it is to obtain them, let's look at it from the perspective of an ant in the road. There's the same desire for happiness, the same desire to be free from suffering. But if we were to try to express even the tiniest speck of our understanding to that animal, we would not succeed. Likewise, how many human beings do you know with whom you can actually share or explain what you know? Circumstantial difficulties do not let people go beyond whatever existence and experiences they're stuck with. Compared with these circumstances, all the little difficulties that impede your path of practice—laziness, having too much to do, and so on—are very tiny and very weak indeed.

Contemplation

Reflect on each of the ten endowments and see whether you are so endowed. At this point, you should be able to realize that all these circumstances have come together within you, and that you truly hold a precious human existence. Contemplating the preciousness of this moment and all of your endowments, generate strong courage within yourself. Generate the courage to establish a ground of meditation strong enough and brave enough to work with all your habitual tendencies, which are just empty thoughts.

5

A Human Birth, So Difficult to Obtain

A HUMAN LIFE IS all the more precious for being so difficult to obtain. The most direct way to look at this is to compare the vast numbers of beings in this very world system. A Tibetan term for sentient beings is *drowa ('gro ba)* which means "movement." Any movement anywhere signifies the presence of a mind, or mental consciousness, and a holder of that mind. The bodies and minds of living beings create the immense amount of movement in all the realms.

Compare the numbers. There are millions and millions of life forms on, above, and below the earth and in the ocean. We think that our human population is huge when actually it is very small compared to the vast numbers of beings in other forms. Just between the human and animal realms—the least populated of the lower realms—there is a vast difference in numbers. Traditionally it's said that the number of beings in the animal realm is equivalent to all the dust particles on the surface of the earth, while human beings equal the number of dust particles on the tip of a needle. Our teachers would tell anyone arrogant enough to boast of the numbers of human beings to dig a pit about four by four feet and look into it carefully. The billions of sentient beings in just that one pit would equal the whole human population.

From that point of view, we must really have a sense of the existence of life forms everywhere—and an appreciation of the vastness of karma and the preciousness of a human existence. There are innumerable beings with no such potential. And of those endowed human beings, how many recognize the cyclic existence of sentient beings and are willing to create the ground of happiness rather than the ground of suffering? How many recognize ignorance and all that arises from it? How many have the opportunities that you and I have to meet with the Dharma and truly put it into practice—and of *those* human beings, how many actually generate motivation and bring their potential to fruition?

Human beings who can truly let go of unvirtuous actions are rare—and rarer still are those who actually put virtuous actions into practice. Since we have this rare potential and opportunity—no matter how weak we are or how many difficulties and habitual tendencies we may have—we have far better circumstances than millions and billions of sentient beings moving about at this particular time.

We must realize how close we actually are to bringing these endowments to fruition—but we're not doing so. A single invisible thought, hesitation, or doubt can cause us to slip, disrupting everything. Not to put our potential to use would be a complete waste of a life. There is no greater waste or deception toward others than to have the ability to generate selflessness but allow distraction to completely destroy you. The understanding that should arise from this is "Do not waste a moment of this life." Do not—through one moment of nonawareness or one emotional obstacle—waste the potential of your higher birth.

Contemplation

From the moment of your birth until now—with all these conditions that so many millions of sentient beings do not have—what have you actually squeezed out as the essence of so many years of life? If you were to die at this moment, what would be the fruition of having had this healthy body and mind and all this potential? What would be left behind, if not for others' benefit then for your own? Endowed with all these qualities, have you ended up just learning and talking about them—as you go about doing the millions of other things you do? Or have you actually planted and nurtured them in your life so they blossom? If this hasn't happened, contemplate the immense waste of mind still unwilling to put this into practice and come to fruition.

Bring awareness to the preciousness of each moment so it can truly arise as the ground of enlightenment. This is the essential meaning of the first reminder, which reminds us *why* we need to exert effort to generate awareness at all times.

A "higher" birth means freedom from samsara, a birth that allows liberation to arise. The cause of such a favorable birth according to the Madhyamika (Middle Way) school of Buddhist teachings is based on ethics, or discipline. In this case, discipline means binding all of our human qualities together with awareness. The binding factor of awareness will bring them to fruition. It will allow us to abandon anything useless or destructive to our human qualities and to cultivate that which will bring them to fruition. Awareness is known as the foundation of liberation, upon which we can bring the eighteen qualities to fruition. What are the benefits of bringing a precious human existence to fruition?

Only a human being can create the favorable ground of karma leading to birth in the higher realms. As a result, this present life could lead to more favorable circumstances in the next—or at the very least a better tomorrow or a better old age. Favorable circumstances can arise only from the ground of positive karma. Fruition depends on a cause; the causes of favorable circumstances are virtuous actions of body, speech, and mind—

and a positive cause cannot be created without awareness. Awareness is the actual discipline that puts positive karma into practice.

We can also talk about lesser and greater fruition. Lesser fruition is the attainment of our own liberation. Individual liberation, or arhatship, is attained through hinayana practices by *arhat*s, known as "solitary realizers." But even this liberation cannot be attained without bringing all eighteen qualities to fruition through the practice of Dharma. The greater fruition is that of a bodhisattva, a fully enlightened compassionate being who benefits all sentient beings. We cannot attain the fruition of a bodhisattva without the cause of a human birth. So no matter what we aspire to—from temporary happiness in this life to the attainment of absolute liberation—the fundamental requirement is a precious human birth endowed with the eighteen qualities.

> Having attained this precious human existence,
> Like a ship that crosses the ocean of samsara,
> Without falling into distractions or laziness of mind
> > through ignorance,
> Allow yourself to awaken to the preciousness of this
> > moment.*

It is not in planning for liberation that liberation arises. Liberation arises from the wakefulness of each moment. This very moment is completely endowed with all the favorable circumstances we need for enlightenment. If and when awareness is *not* generated, it's only because we're unaware of these fundamental qualities—which therefore are not fully utilized. The importance of strengthening awareness is understood from contemplating impermanence, the second thought that transforms the mind.

* From the *Bodhicharyavatara,* by Shantideva. Translated by the author from Tibetan.

PART Two

Second Thought: Impermanence

The three realms are as impermanent as autumn clouds.
The births and deaths of beings are like a dance perform-
ance.
Flashing by like lightning in the sky, the life span of beings
Races swiftly like a waterfall over a steep mountain.

To understand impermanence correctly, we must acknowledge the fact that we are all going to die. We all
know that we will die—and we all have a tendency to ob-
scure that awareness and to hope that we will not. Our
awareness of the certainty of death and the hope of being
the one exception give rise to laziness; laziness arises
when there is some hope that either we can ignore death
or we won't have to go through it when the time comes.
Laziness prevents our precious human qualities from
being put to use. The antidote to this and other habitual
tendencies is the contemplation of impermanence. Resting the mind on reminders of impermanence, we can see
that everything we're attached to or hold dear is subject
to change.

6

The Great Impermanence of Death

THE BUDDHA TAUGHT that death comes because of life. In the same way, sickness comes where there is health, old age comes where there is youth, destruction comes where there is construction. This logic establishes the law of existence itself—and meditators must not only understand this, they must be able to put it into practice.

The actual fact of death cannot be denied. Even individuals endowed with a precious human existence are subject to impermanence and death. No matter how far we travel in the ten directions, we won't find anyone who has not experienced this. The simplest mind can understand that nothing remains the same: there is constant generation, degeneration, transformation, and change. All of our experiences—of people, places, and other outer phenomena as well as inner thoughts and feelings—are impermanent. A mind that does not genuinely understand this provides the ground for distraction and habitual patterns.

It takes a genuine sense of urgency to use this very moment to bring our positive endowments to fruition. For this we must actually have some feeling for the *experience* of impermanence.

Reflecting on the impermanence of all phenomena should truly give rise to a sense of fear—not a paralyzing fear that keeps us from generating positive tendencies or bringing our potential to fruition, but a genuine sense of urgency in the face of impermanence.

Just as change and impermanence arise in infinite ways, so too death arises. Death arising as impermanence can be caused by any number of things. There may not be any one cause that disrupts a life or causes death. There are also many different experiences of impermanence given the various life spans of sentient beings. The Tibetan tradition talks about life spans from thousands of years long to those in the degenerate age that can be as short as ten years, a few days, or less. Contemplate the infinite numbers of beings that are going through a vast variety of experiences based on the fruition of their karma.

If the urgency of impermanence still does not arise, think of examples from your personal experience. Think of all the people you've known who are no longer with you today. How many of these relatives or friends have actually passed away? In *The Words of My Perfect Teacher,* Patrul Rinpoche talks about all of the realized teachers and great meditators who nevertheless have been subject to impermanence and are no longer alive today. When you light your shrine and hang beautiful pictures of your teachers, keep in mind that impermanence hits everyone, even those to whom you've done prostrations. Then relate this understanding to the impermanence of other circumstances in your life.

We can see that every movement is a step closer to death. Simple acts such as eating, walking, or sitting down bring us closer to the exhaustion of these experiences and closer to death. We may tell ourselves that a human life span is seventy or eighty years, but each month and year marks the passage of time. And regardless of our life span, death can strike at any moment. We could calculate the time that has passed and the time that remains, but even if we were sure we had that much time left, there is less of it with each passing moment—and it's not possible to add on any time. Given the fact of ever less time and our approaching old age—when we will truly experience impermanence—why would we still succumb to distractions and hesitations?

When we look back at the time of death, the experience of this life will seem like a dream. And—just as with our nighttime dreams—it will seem useless to have put so much effort into it. The fear we experience in a dream is gone when we wake up; feeling afraid was just an unnecessary exertion of effort causing us to lose sleep! When we look back on our lives at death, the amount of time we spent in hesitation, aggression, ignorance, selfishness, jealousy, hatred, self-preservation, and arrogance will seem like an equally useless exertion of energy. So be able to regard all these illusory thoughts and concepts as dreams. Within this illusory existence, what, if anything, is the logic behind any stubbornness, distraction, hesitation, or habitual emotions of aggression, desire, selfishness, and jealousy? What is the use of holding on to these useless emotions within impermanence? Impermanence is the nature of everything.

Contemplation

Begin your contemplation with the awareness that even the ground you are sitting on is subject to change. Ask yourself if you have ever seen or met any sentient being on, above, or below this earth who has not experienced death. If the answer is no, sit in meditation with the awareness that you too will experience impermanence. Even your view and understanding and all the effort you put into thinking about things—beneficial or not, distracted or awake—is impermanent. Contemplate the impermanence and death of everything inside and outside you as much as possible.

Then think of all the time wasted in distractedness, non-awareness, hesitation, and sleep—and in simply waiting for the right circumstances. Add to that the number of years that have already passed and the number of years you will spend in such states in the future. How much time do you actually have left to regard this life as a dream?

Impermanence lurks in all conceivable and inconceivable causes. An outer cause such as medicine could be life-sustaining or the cause of death. Natural elements such as earth, water, fire, or wind and other external phenomena such as mountains and trees could cause one's death. Inner circumstances such as illness and our own doubts, hesitations, and thoughts themselves can arise as the cause of death. All such outer and inner phenomena have the full potential to cause impermanence and death.

Impermanence is the fruition of all of the impermanent causes, or karma, we've created. The Buddha himself explained that everything that originates from a cause—every perception, movement, and form—must inevitably be left behind at the moment of death. Other than our own karma, we take nothing with us at the moment of death. No matter how strong our grasping and attachment, we cannot take our material wealth, physical body, friends, relatives, teachers, retinues, or disciples. No matter how many dear ones surround us in this life wanting never to be separated from us; no matter what our rank or power; no matter how much effort we've put into cultivating a home, a position, or knowledge, oratorical, and debating skills, none of it can be brought into the experience of death.

Trying to maintain anything at the moment of death adds nothing to our time or happiness—and it does not allow for the simplicity of letting go. It does not allow us to have a sense of accomplishment at the time of death or to be the cause of happiness for anyone else.

Understanding this, why do we still grasp at material possessions and all our other attachments? Grasping and attachment can survive only in a mind where there is still some hope: "Maybe someday it will be possible to take a little something with me—if not these samsaric things, at least a little something Buddhist: my devotions, teachers, teachings, ritual objects." Nothing, however, can be brought into death other than the simple cause and effect of our accumulated karma and the transcendence of our mind and view—to the extent that view is truly useful.

7

The Wisdom of Discernment

IN THE BUDDHIST SUTRAS, we find that the Buddha's students requested him not to enter into *mahaparinirvana*. At that point, the Buddha gave his most essential teaching on the experience of death. The essence of the instruction is this: Everything that is born dies; everything that is generated goes through degeneration and destruction.

We can do no greater harm to ourselves than not to think about impermanence. Where impermanence is not properly understood, everything samsaric becomes important and a seemingly reasonable cause to accomplish, when in fact life is as fragile as a bubble. We cannot really say whether the next moment will bring the experience of the next moment or the next life. In the time between inhaling and exhaling, we cannot guarantee that breath will not stop. The causes of impermanence and death are many; at this very moment, we could do something to cause destruction or death to arise. We cannot really plan ahead as far as tomorrow, let alone the next ten or twenty years.

If the mind is obscured by ignorance at the time of death, it will create more ignorance. If we respond to the experience of impermanence with complete openness and selflessness, however, our understanding will be the foundation of liberation from suffering.

Contemplating impermanence gives rise to the wisdom of discernment. With this we can truly discern between useful activities that bring about genuine goodness and useless activities that are of no benefit to anyone. Seeing the enormous amount of time and energy we spend in useless activities, we can turn our mind toward Dharma, which is an activity that is truly fruitful and beneficial for sentient beings.

Contemplation

In such a fragile and changing existence, what distraction, laziness, or ignorance is important enough to dismantle the awareness needed to rest in your fundamental nature? Contemplating impermanence, focus your mind on this: If death occurs at this moment, what is most essential? What will truly benefit yourself and others? Will any of the concepts, hesitations, or distractions that you allow to rule your life truly make any sense at the moment of death? And if holding on to such things won't help you or anyone else at that moment, why would any sensible human being with such precious endowments continue to be enslaved by them?

At this moment, you have the potential for control. You can take this opportunity to bring your potential to fruition. To do this, you must let go of any stubbornness and grasping at notions of solidity where there is none—and bring whatever arises into genuine awareness inseparable from buddha mind, your enlightened essence.

It is not only in death that we see constant change: time is constantly changing; thoughts are constantly changing. Constant movement prevents the mind from ever coming to rest with complete certainty that it is not subject to impermanence. Nevertheless, we continue to assume that time is solid, thoughts are solid, our movements are solid, and this "self" is solid. Mistaking that which is impermanent to be permanent, we come up with a mistaken view, based on which we try to solidify things that are constantly in flux.

Time is a simple example of this. We usually think of time in terms of past, present, and future time. Each of these notions requires the existence of one moment that stays still. We base our solid sense of time on a single solid moment called present time, and any other moment is past or future. Proving this, however, is impossible, since there is no such thing as "present time." The stream of time is constantly changing and not solid: as soon as we think of the present it is already past.

In the same way, thoughts are constantly in flux. As soon as we think a certain thought—and then busily base our judgments on it—its inner essence has already moved on. The movement of the initial thought creates a second thought; and by the time we recognize it, the second thought arises as a third thought, and so on.

And what about this seemingly solid self? Nagarjuna describes how even the great and massive civilizations of this earth are completely dismantled, changed, and, impermanent as dust particles, blown away by the wind. Whole world systems collide and collapse and become extinct. Compared to that, any arrogance based on the seeming solidity of a single, impermanent self would be quite unnecessary and a mark of ignorance.

But we have come to believe in the solidity of our emotions and to base our judgments on them. From the belief in a solid self—which can't even be posited from the standpoint of impermanence—grasping and the logic of grasping arise. Because we think we have cause for grasping and an object to grasp, endless displays of selfishness and emotions create further distraction from the fundamental ground. We will continue to generate selfishness and unkindness as long as we maintain some cause: jealousy has a cause, hatred has a cause, aggression has a cause. These are the depths of ignorance to which the minds of sentient beings can go.

Although selfishness has no actual cause or location, we still feel that ultimately, somewhere inside, there's a secure storeroom where attachment is quietly hidden and all of the things we want to hold on to are stacked and inventoried. But if everything is in a constant state of flux, what could we possibly find to protect or maintain? And how could we possibly "store" anything? All of the emotional displays that we try to maintain are nothing but suppositions of mind—a mind that hasn't understood change.

Contemplation

Allow your mind to go further into a sense of death arising in each passing moment. Every move you make is an indication of change and impermanence. Each moment you sit in meditation, manifold degeneration, destruction, and change take place. In light of this, any tendency to still feel separate from impermanence and change would be absolute ignorance, which would prevent clear understanding from arising in the mind. Remain in meditation with a genuine awareness of constant impermanence and the urgency arising from this.

If impermanence is true, however, we can actually give rise to positive tendencies. If change is the very nature of all outer and inner phenomena, there is no basis for any confidence in a solid self and no need for any logic to defend or protect it. Why then would we generate anger, for example? Anger is generated solely to protect a self that has to retain its identity and defend its ground—a self that is not really there. Contemplating our various experiences of impermanence, we can understand how unnecessary and useless it is to grasp at a self—at which point genuine selflessness arises.

8

Training in Awareness

T HE REAL INTENT behind any Dharma practice is to train the mind for the moment of death so that the moment of death can arise with confidence and without regret—regret in the sense of nonawareness, or ignorance. As we develop awareness, we get a better understanding of the very subtle thoughts that constantly shift the mind into nonawareness.

Lacking awareness, we are unable to understand impermanence and the emptiness of thought, time, and a self—empty in the sense that they cannot be proven to exist. Imposing solidity upon that inherently empty nature, we spend whole lifetimes struggling with ourselves and others. When we look at all the sentient beings living like this, we can truly understand how difficult it is to become free from suffering in the midst of samsara.

The only way to free yourself from ignorance is the path of awareness. Training in awareness begins with you. It would be difficult to go outside of yourself to get this message—or to change the mind of anyone else. You are the one endowed with the qualities, teachings, and practices; you are the one with the genuine desire and ability to bring this to fruition. Therefore, you need to be the first one to transcend ignorance. Then and only then can you benefit others. This is the reason we contemplate impermanence.

Knowing that all sentient beings desire happiness, we are unable to generate happiness because of nonawareness. How can we overcome suffering? How can we gain happiness and be the cause of happiness when the basis of our every action is completely contradictory to that? In a single moment, there can be so many stains of ignorance and shades of hesitation. If we're awake enough to recognize these subtle shifts, we will find that the "big things" we think of as the cause of samsara—gross emotions of anger, ignorance, desire, hatred, and so forth—are not really the problem. They are second- or third-hand results of nonawareness, which is the core essence of distraction.

Recognizing that shift is called training the mind. For this, we emphasize training in meditation (see appendix A). The point of your meditation—or devotion or practice of any kind—is a clean, precise understanding of the *subtle* shifts of mind that generate the gross emotions of ignorance, desire, or hatred. Recognizing this, you will be able to maintain clear awareness.

⊚ *Contemplation*

What matters most in meditation is the quality, not the duration, of your practice. You could spend hours in meditation still enveloped in a contaminated view of something to hold on to, an identity to maintain, and the same habitual grasping. This is just pretense, just the form of meditation, and not the genuine transcendence of mind. If you sit for only five minutes, see if you can remain within mindfulness and compassion completely free from self-grasping for those five minutes.

The path of awareness begins with the Four Reminders. Think carefully about impermanence and the preciousness of human existence, and not just in terms of "Yes, this is true, yes that happens." Otherwise, you'll spend your life saying, "Of course everything is impermanent," and "Yes, he or she is dead," and "Of course I'm not confident that when I breathe out I'll breathe in again." This kind of belief is not what we are talking about; these are just *clues* or steps to contemplation.

The important thing is to reach a point where our hearts are truly shaken by a genuine sense of fear—fear in the sense that impermanence arises with every moment. This brings a starkly naked awareness of just how *silly* this great arrogance is that we have about "my" life: my views, my understanding, my hopes and fears. When that shift of the heart actually happens, we will glimpse for the first time the real importance of all the teachings and instructions. And from then on, we will not need anyone else to tell us about the truth of impermanence. This is the kind of confidence we need as an antidote to distraction and all its emotional and conceptual displays.

It is most unlikely that we will ever understand the real intent of Dharma or practice, however, until our mind matures through proper contemplation of the Four Reminders. In the Buddhist tradition, the Four Reminders are contemplated often. You will find some reference to them before every practice session and at the beginning of every single text in all 84,000 tenets and commentaries. The point of contemplating the Four Reminders is to see who and what we are as human beings: we are completely endowed with enlightened potential, and we completely embody impermanence and karma. This is what we can be proud of, and this is what we can be not so proud of—but this *is* what we are.

It is entirely up to us to work with this—either from the point of view of awareness, which leads to nirvana, or from that of ignorance, which leads to samsara. This is the reasoning behind samsara and nirvana, existence and enlightenment. Because of our inherent buddha nature, the choice is always ours. The only question is whether we choose the path of wisdom or the path of ignorance.

There is no reason for anyone to go willingly into ignorance when there is wisdom. Remaining within wisdom—using any support that best brings this about—is the life of a Buddhist practitioner. If being spiritual and using spiritual terms inspires you, then by all means add the Buddha and all the Buddhist teachings to your life. If it inspires you to simply be who you are and practice as you are without any spiritual terminology, that's fine too. The essential thing is to get down to using your life properly.

Contemplating the preciousness of human life and the impermanence of all things brings us to the next reminder, the suffering of the six realms of existence.

BUSINESS REPLY MAIL

FIRST-CLASS MAIL PERMIT NO. 11494 BOSTON MA

POSTAGE WILL BE PAID BY ADDRESSEE

SHAMBHALA PUBLICATIONS
PO BOX 170358
BOSTON MA 02117-9812

SHAMBHALA PUBLICATIONS

If you'd like to receive a copy of our latest catalogue of books and audios, please fill out and return this card. It's easy—the postage is already paid!

Or, if you'd prefer, you can e-mail us at CustomerCare@shambhala.com, sign up online at www.shambhala.com/newsletter, or call toll-free (888) 424-2329.

NAME

ADDRESS

CITY / STATE / ZIP / COUNTRY

E-MAIL

And by also giving us your e-mail address, you'll automatically be signed up to receive news about new releases, author events, and special offers!

Third Thought: The Suffering of the Six Realms

Overpowered by existence, craving, and ignorance,
All beings—humans, gods, and beings of the three lower
  realms—
Circle unwittingly in the five realms* of existence
Like the spinning of a potter's wheel.

With the understanding of the truth of impermanence
and the inevitability of death comes another very important realization: our next experience will arise as the
fruition of the karma we create at this moment. This
brings us to the third reminder, the suffering of the six
realms of existence.

---

* Editor's note: Because the god and asura realms are sometimes
counted as one, the six realms may be listed as five realms.

9

The Six Realms of Existence and Karma

MOST HUMAN BEINGS, no matter how good our intentions, do not understand the suffering of others. It is difficult even to imagine the kinds of suffering described in Buddhist texts. Yet we aspire to selfless compassion for all sentient beings. Without a proper understanding of suffering, however, it's difficult to practice selflessness—and boasting of selfless compassion would be a lie. Unbiased compassion must be based on an unbiased understanding of suffering that completely encompasses all sentient beings.

What is a sentient being? All sentient beings have the capacity to move and to desire, if nothing else, happiness instead of suffering. No being wants to experience pain or to be taken from its existence, which—no matter how bad it may seem to us—is just as important to that being as our own is to us.

What is suffering? For most of us, it's the feeling that our wishes aren't being fulfilled or that not everyone likes us, listens to us, or does what we want them to do. It's painful and we call it suffering. Some of us suffer a bit more with the pain of disease, divorce, or bankruptcy. We may suffer the loss of a job or fail to find the right husband or wife. This does not compare to true suffering, however. If we were to see suffering for what it truly is, we would be genuinely shaken—and from that moment on, we'd have no problem with revulsion toward the six realms and no further attachment to them.

Consider, therefore, the kindness of all the teachers who have put into words the manifold suffering of sentient beings. Most of us have never truly experienced this kind of suffering—or the sense of urgency that arises from it. Therefore, we still make excuses. So many things seem to carry more weight than freedom from suffering and wanting others to be free from suffering.

Because of ignorance, sentient beings are unable to create good karma or abandon negative karma. For this reason alone, no matter how much we hope for happiness, happiness will not come. And no matter how much we don't want to suffer, the suffering of samsara will continue. Contemplating the six realms, we understand that samsara is suffering and suffering is created by sentient beings. When we understand the immensely diverse ways we create and experience suffering, we will realize the importance of creating the ground of positive karma upon which liberation can come to fruition.

Contemplation

As a meditator, relax the stubbornness of your mind and extend your mind beyond what your senses can perceive. Appreciate the presence of millions of living beings in whatever forms they exist. There are sentient beings as big as mountains and others so small they cannot be seen with our eyes. Each of them possesses a body and mind with hopes, fears, and the aspiration to sustain its existence. Each one creates karma that comes to fruition as a particular samsaric environment, and each one desires happiness and freedom from suffering. In spite of this, all of them are stuck in ignorance and unable to recognize that the ground of happiness is created from positive karma. Contemplate their immeasurable sufferings—which are more than you can read about or understand.

The six realms are divided into three lower and three upper realms. The lower realms are the hell, hungry ghost, and animal realms. The upper realms are the human, jealous god, and god realms. There are many different explanations of these realms, but I'm aware of none more clear and direct than Patrul Rinpoche's in *The Words of My Perfect Teacher*, where each realm is described as a particular experience of suffering.

Some people think of the six realms as psychological or imaginary states. And some even try to include all six realms within the human-realm experience. They think, for example, that the human experience of extreme hunger and thirst is the same as hungry ghost–realm suffering; or that our experiences of extreme violence, warfare, or pain are real hell-realm situations; or that any great comfort, joy, wealth, and luxury are actually god realms—all within our own world system. But we should not mistake these human experiences for the six realms themselves. Our experiences of extreme poverty, hunger, and thirst are human, not hungry ghost sufferings. A war-torn country or some other disastrous situation with violence, aggression, and negative tendencies toward extreme pain should not be mistaken for the hell realm. Experiences of extreme pain and suffering are part of this human realm.

A popular topic these days is whether or not distinct realms actually exist. It's really not useful or necessary to say anything more than simply that they do exist—just as this realm exists. We see it, we believe in it, we have our human-realm experiences. Similarly, most of us can understand the animal realm; we can see how these beings create their realm. The other realms are just as easy to understand if we work through our understanding of cause and effect. From one moment of distracted grasping, karma is created that comes to fruition as a particular kind of experience—with all its emotions, perceptions, and formations—and a particular environment.

Each karma, or action, has a particular result for the individual who creates it. It also has an effect on the environment and the limitless relationships that person has with others. So your own accumulated karma affects you, the environment, and other sentient beings, and their accumulated karma affects them, the environment, and you.

In this way, anything—subtle or gross—can be created. Just as we've created this human experience, other sentient beings have created other situations. So, the six realms are a complete description of samsara, and our experience of the realms is the fruition of our karma. Based on karmic fruition, we are now experiencing the human realm. When our bodies die, our mind consciousnesses will move on and mingle with the force of the karma we're accumulating now. This will result in a particular kind of experience and environment or world system.

It may seem difficult at first to logically prove the presence of a hell realm, for example. We may feel we'd like to take a camera or camcorder into the hell realm and bring back a record of the experience. Questions arise about the kinds of karma that lead to the realms into which we're born. We can work with these questions as we go along. The important thing to remember is that death *will* occur—and before it does, we should really pause and contemplate exactly what we've accumulated in terms of karma.

The Three Lower Realms

LOOKING AT THE DIFFERENT KINDS of births that are pos-sible based on accumulated karma, we see that intensely negative karma leads to birth in the three lower realms: the ani-mal, hungry ghost, and hell realms. Where negative karma is less intense, it arises—depending on the *kind* of karma—as birth in the three upper realms: the god, jealous god, and human realms. All six realms are within the samsaric cycle of existence, and none of them is free from suffering or the cause of suffering. To un-derstand them better, we'll look first at the three lower realms, beginning with the hell realms.

The Hell Realms

Just as good karma comes to fruition, negative karma comes to fruition—like it or not. A karmic fruition such as a hell realm should not be seen as a punishment. This is not the case at all. The Tibetan word *nyalwa* (*dmyal ba*), or "hell realm," simply refers to the fruition of painfulness: it's the arising of painful experiences caused by the karma of creating pain. Any sense of "fault" here is the fault of nonawareness. When a human being—endowed with the ability to abandon unvirtuous actions—intentionally or unintentionally doesn't make that perfect choice, a karmic seed is planted that results in some painful experience. If we sum up all the pain we could possibly experience into one realm, that realm would be called a hell realm. The karma that creates such an experience is said to be intense fear at the time of death.

At the time of death, negative karma usually creates an experience of great fear, great regret, or utter confusion. This is due to the complete groundlessness of the experience and our inability to make any sense of it. The one thing human beings truly feel sure of is the ground. When we lift our foot, we're sure the ground will still be there when we put it down. We use "the ground under our feet" as a metaphor to describe certainty, something that no one can challenge. That certainty becomes a solid comfort zone that we return to again and again. A sense of stubbornness or rigidity develops as ego grasps at its solid ground.

Grasping at solidity is like grasping at the ground of aggression or any other habitual tendency. We know that aggression is negative; nevertheless, it's familiar ground—as is our knowing how bad it is. These familiar things create our ground of experience. We may not like our habitual tendencies, but we revert to them again and again as familiar ground, and every moment of our life is based on the certainty of that ground.

At the time of death—ready and willing or not—our ground is taken away. Fear or confusion can arise as our sense of solidity dissolves along with the four elements that make up this physical body. With the dissolution of the elements, the body no longer has any ground; mind and thoughts are no longer there either, no matter how hard we try to cling to them. This experience is said to be like drowning. The fear in a drowning person's mind generates an action: trying to hold on to water. Similarly, the dying person tries to hold on to something, anything—beliefs, wishes, the faith one has held on to all one's life—to no avail.

At the moment of death, nothing remains and every bit of

ground that has supported our identity collapses. The destruction of our ground can give rise to confusion, fear, and regret—along with the actual experience of death, which is said to be like falling into a deep sleep. When the exhaustion of mind and body is complete—just as we would arise from a deep sleep and become aware of the external environment—we arise as a mental awareness with an immense sense of groundlessness. That moment is described as a state of complete bewilderment, which becomes the ground for the fruition of the backlog of karma accumulated throughout previous lifetimes.

The moment the bewildered state is hit by the intensity of all that previous karma, the next realm and our next life experience are born. If the power of accumulated karma is based on negative actions—harmfulness, killing, or other heinous crimes—it will produce a negative fruition. The logic is simple: when the seed is sour, the fruit is sour, and when the seed is sweet, the fruit is sweet. A negative karmic seed produces suffering and pain, which we will experience as birth in a lower realm such as a hot or cold hell realm. There are actually eighteen hell realms from our human point of view: eight hot hells, eight cold hells, the neighboring hells, and the ephemeral hell. Each has its own environment, depending on the karma of those who create it.

Contemplation

Use the creative abilities of your mind to reflect on these particular kinds of suffering. The mind is able to create enormous concepts; use that skill to create not only the beautiful things you'd like to believe in but also the things that are difficult. Contemplate the creation of all the karma leading to such experiences. Going beyond that, let your mind understand the totality of suffering. To generate compassion for all sentient beings, we must include the sentient beings experiencing the intense pain described here.

We will look first at the eight hot hells. Whereas the human realm is composed mainly of four elements—earth, water, fire, and wind—the hot hells are mainly made of fire. Their descriptions in the texts as "filled with fire and intensely hot," where "molten lava is poured down one's throat," fail to capture the real pain there. A fierce fire element, 100,000 times more intense than the fire in our human realm, makes up the entire environment. The heat and burning are said to be even more intense than the world colliding with the sun. The eight hot hells are named for the intensity of their suffering.

The first hot hell, known as the Reviving Hell, is made entirely of flames in all ten directions. Here, due to the accumulated karma of being involved with weapons or harmful devices, we view others with a sense of great hatred. The anger in our minds is visited upon us with a thousand times more aggression. Combined with the karma of weaponry, this tremendous aggression causes us—in spite of our own inconceivably intense pain and suffering—to inflict harm on others. We continue to harm others based on the karma of the realm itself, which is described as a wind that continually blows everything back into form. So we experience ongoing death and revival and hatred of others, which creates ongoing aggression.

To think that karma is created only in *this* life and merely comes to fruition in the other realms is a misunderstanding of the enormous implications of karma. Karma refers to a cause, its fruition, and further limitless creations. The hell realms, like other realms, are places where karma not only comes to fruition but also is created. When we are stuck in the six realms, we experience a continuous cycle of suffering—which is why samsaric existence is said to spin like a wheel, with no beginning or end.

THE SECOND HOT HELL is a realm of even more intense suffering known as the Black Mark Hell. Here our body is marked and then cut into pieces. Our teachers used to describe this very graphically. They would talk about how the saw is extremely rusty and not very sharp, how it has to be pushed and pulled, and how it takes hundreds of years just for the cutting—during which time we are completely conscious.

There are sentient beings with a capacity for pain beyond the limits of what we know or want to know. In our own limited experience, a small cut can cause us to lose consciousness. A human being is endowed with very small, limited body and a mind that is also somewhat limited. Although our potential is great, our capacity for the intensity of experience is gentler. Because of this human gentleness, we may greatly underestimate the physical and mental experiences of other beings. Beings in the hell or preta realms have vast bodies and minds—as vast, some texts say, as this universe itself. With such vastness, the intensity of pain is that much greater.

THE THIRD HOT HELL is the Crushing Hell, where as soon as we become aware of our environment, our body is crushed between two mountains—which often arise in the form of lions, tigers, sheep, and other animals. Due to the karma of inflicting harm or taking life, we perceive these beings in enormous forms, such as large mountains, rising up to attack or kill us. When the mountains separate, we're revived, only to go through the same experience again and again.

THE FOURTH HOT HELL is the Crying Hell, where the pain and suffering of extreme heat is so intense that we can do nothing but cry out aloud. Intensely afraid, we run around trying to escape but find nothing but a great metal house or dome. Entering that, we're sealed in, and for countless years our body is burned until there is no experience of a body at all, as it has completely turned into fire.

THE FIFTH HOT HELL is called the Greater Crying Hell because the suffering is said to be twice that of the Crying Hell.

THE SIXTH HOT HELL is known as the Heating Hell. Here we have the physical experience of being roasted alive, until the sense of the body itself exceeds the limits of the sky and the experience of body and flames is inseparable.

THE SEVENTH HOT HELL is the Intense Heating Hell, where the intensity of flames is double that of the previous realm. Our body is pierced with flaming rods, and we are subjected to such extreme burning that we become inseparable from the flames.

THE EIGHTH AND LOWEST HOT HELL is *avici* hell, or the Hell of Ceaseless Torment. Committing any of the five heinous crimes or, as a vajrayana practitioner, developing adverse views regarding the vajra master causes birth in this hell realm. The five heinous crimes that bring immediate retribution are: killing one's father, killing one's mother, killing an arhat, malevolently causing a buddha to bleed, and creating a schism within the Dharma community. Here one's skin, bone, marrow, and so on become a fire so intense that a whole world system could be immediately and completely turned to dust just coming into contact with it. Except for cries of suffering, there is no indication of the presence of physical bodies. It is as if one's entire existence is reduced to a mass of burning and incessant torment.

This is the suffering of sentient beings at this very moment, and the duration of their suffering is difficult to imagine. Based on our human-realm understanding of time, fifty human years equals one day in the god realm of the Four Great Kings; and five hundred years in this god realm equals one day in the first hot hell, the Reviving Hell, where beings suffer for five hundred such years. As for the second hell realm, the Black Mark Hell, one hundred human years equals one day in the god realm of the Thirty-three Devas; and a thousand years in this god realm equals one day in the second hell realm, where beings suffer for a thousand such years. In this way, the duration of suffering in the hell realms multiplies with each successive realm until the eighth hot hell, where the suffering lasts for one kalpa. Simply put, sentient beings spend an inconceivable amount of time in the hell realms. To really understand samsara for what it is, we must understand this—even if it seems difficult or completely beyond our comprehension.

The second group of hell realms is made up of eight cold hells. Here, just as hot hells are made of fire, the environment is made of the elements wind and water—and, of course, extreme cold.

THE FIRST COLD HELL is known as the Hell of Blisters. We are born here completely naked, surrounded by snow blizzards and ice. The cold is a thousand times greater than our human understanding of cold. Left alone without any sense of support or courage, we experience such intense cold that our entire body breaks out in blisters.

THE SECOND COLD HELL is known as the Hell of Bursting Blisters. Because the cold is a thousand times more intense than the first cold hell, the blisters all burst and are completely devoured by various insects and animals, giving rise to an intensity of pain beyond our comprehension.

IN THE THIRD COLD HELL, the Hell of Clenched Teeth, the cold is so intense that the teeth of the beings are tightly clenched.

IN THE FOURTH COLD HELL, the Hell of Lamentations, the intense pain of cold and fear and suffering causes beings born here to lament and cry out ceaselessly.

THE FIFTH COLD HELL is called the Groaning Hell. Here the intensity of pain is so great that even speech is not possible and beings simply groan with the suffering of intense cold.

IN THE SIXTH COLD HELL, known as the Hell of Utpalalike Cracks, the experience of pain becomes ever greater as one's skin turns blue and splits into four petal-like pieces resembling the *utpala* flower.

THE SEVENTH AND EIGHTH COLD HELLS are described as the Hell of Lotuslike Cracks and the Hell of Great Lotuslike Cracks. This refers to a cold so intense that our entire body turns red and simply bursts into pieces resembling a lotus—first four pieces, like a four-petaled lotus, and then many pieces, like a many-petaled lotus.

A life span in the cold hells is described in the treasury of teachings as the length of time it would take to empty a great hundred-kilo urn filled to the brim with mustard seeds, if a single seed were taken out every hundred years. This would be the life span of beings in the first cold hell; for the other cold hells, multiply by twenty urns, forty urns, and so on.

Again, we need to understand the enormity of samsara and not limit it to our own small fears, aggressions, doubts, or hesitations—which sometimes seem so enormous. Samsara is not just our little world or the emotions we struggle with or the difficulties we have with our spiritual practice. Samsara is an inconceivable number of sentient beings and all their diverse realms, experiencing tremendous suffering for vast expanses of time—

compared to which our concept of time is very tiny. Imagine meeting someone who's lived for millions of years in a hell realm and saying to this being, "I can't meditate because of laziness." How irrelevant would that seem to someone experiencing such suffering?

The point of contemplating the hell realms is not just to develop a fear of karma or to look at the many ways our lives can take form. The point is to see the enormity of our potential to create samsara and all its manifestations. Then we can see there's no place in this mind for any kind of arrogance or pride or stubbornness.

A THIRD CLASS OF HELLS known as neighboring hells surrounds the Hell of Ceaseless Torment in the four directions. In the intermediate directions are hills of iron *shalmali* trees. The four neighboring hells are called Pit of Embers, Swamp of Decaying Corpses, Plain of Razors, and Forest of Swords. Here's how they work.

After a kalpa of exhausting our karma in the Hell of Ceaseless Torment, we come out of that realm. But no matter which direction we go in, we encounter a neighboring hell. Coming out of a burning hell, we may see the cool shadows of a forest. Having been deprived of such coolness and peace for thousands of years, we rush toward it—but as soon as we reach it, it changes into fire and great weapons that pierce the body through and through. In another direction we might see a cool stream and run toward it, only to have it change into a stream of decaying corpses in which we drown. With intense fear and regret, we express thousands of emotions that intensify our pain.

We might also experience being pierced and shredded as we respond to something known as karmic imprint, which is the sight of relatives and other familiar faces. This karmic imprint pertains especially to monks and nuns who have broken vows of chastity. Patrul Rinpoche describes it like this: You're at the base of a mountain looking up, where you see friends and family calling you. As you rush up the mountain, each rock, bush, and blade of grass turns into a weapon. In spite of being pierced and in pain, you continue to climb. Shredded to pieces, you arrive at the top, but nothing is there. Looking down the mountain, you see your family and friends at the base. Again you rush toward them, with the same painful result—for thousands and thousands of years. This example shows the power of karmic imprint to pull us, in spite of intense pain.

Even when we know something is bad for us, a karmic imprint can lure us into continuing to harm ourselves. A negative thought, for example, might be undermining our basic sanity and destroying our life. Nevertheless, we allow ourselves to be pulled in and destroyed by the force of a grasping mind. Because of the pull of something as simple as an empty thought, we continue to harm ourselves in spite of intense pain—just as we do when we see our relatives or friends. We remain in these neighboring hell realms for a time that's impossible to calculate in terms of human life.

THE FOURTH CATEGORY OF HELLS is known as the ephemeral hells. The beings here are the only hell-realm beings that can be found in the human realm. They may be born in the ocean, earth, rocks, or the many other places where various kinds of beings may live. Their suffering in these various conditions is very intense because every experience bounces back as a reaction a million times greater in magnitude. Their experience of pain, for example, is a million times greater than ours. For example, the consciousness of innumerable such beings could be born within a burning campfire—in the rocks, wood, and the fire itself—where they would experience being completely burned. They could be embedded in the rocks we walk on or in an ordinary glass, table, or door. Any harsh action or sound, such as slamming the door, would cause them intense fear and pain. Trapped in such circumstances for countless lifetimes, they experience the overwhelming fear of being subjected to intense pain inflicted by others at any time.

If the hell realms astound us, we must think about never creating the ground that gives rise to them. The only way to avoid the tremendous suffering of hot and cold, fear and pain is to bring awareness to our actions in this life. As long as there is still life in this body and mind, we can still create the ground of freedom from samsaric suffering—and generate compassion for the limitless sentient beings trapped in it. May the effort you exert in your practice arise as the cause of their freedom. May your awareness and realization arise as the ability to free them.

The Hungry Ghost Realm

The second of the six realms is known as the hungry ghost (*preta*) realm. While aggression and anger are the main cause of hell realms, the main cause of the hungry ghost realm is selfishness and stinginess, or a lack of generosity. Like hell-realm beings, hungry ghosts can experience a variety of suffering, but their main suffering is intense hunger and thirst.

In the hungry ghost realm, our hunger and thirst are so intense that the entire body shrivels up until it no longer resembles a body. The throat is said to be as narrow or fine as a thin needle—but the belly is as vast as the sky. Because no amount of food and water can pass through this narrow throat or fill such a belly, we're completely unable to satisfy our hunger and thirst. The intensity of ongoing hunger and thirst render us completely incapable of moving.

In the distance, we see a lake full of water and many different kinds of fruit and food, but we're unable to move toward them. Nevertheless, we make an intense effort, struggling with all our might for hundreds of years. When we finally reach that body of water and wonderful food, the lake dries up and the food turns to dust. Our extreme suffering is doubled by the nearness of food and water that can't be consumed. This gives rise to the further suffering of great regret. Our mind is very clear and we're absolutely aware of the karma that led to this birth. These are said to be the outer experiences of sentient beings in the hungry ghost realm.

The inner experiences of hungry ghosts are also described. Again, with a mouth as small as the eye of a needle and a belly as vast as a mountain, we spend hundreds of thousands of lifetimes trying to satisfy the burning pangs of hunger and thirst. If, after all our effort, we should manage to consume a drop of water, we cannot feel it in the vastness of such a stomach. And if we do experience that drop of water, it turns into molten lava, inflicting even more harm and pain. This is the experience of the inner obscurations leading to the hungry ghost realm.

Furthermore, hungry ghosts are physically more delicate than human beings. Their body texture is so fine that any heat or cold is experienced 100,000 times more intensely than it is by human beings. So a hungry ghost's entire being is made up of suffering. A life span in this realm is said to last until the negative karma of being born here is exhausted. This could take hundreds of thousands of years. Centuries of wandering in incessant torment may pass without so much as a drop of water or a grain of food.

The Animal Realm

The third of the six realms is the animal realm. This is an existence of great ignorance, fear, and pain. There are many kinds of animals, and they all suffer from complete ignorance and lack of control over their lives. Killing and eating one another, the powerful attacking the weak, the weak gathering to harm others, great ignorance rendering them unable to protect themselves, and intense and constant fear—these are the various sufferings that animals experience.

In cold weather or a storm, for example, even an incapable human being can at least seek shelter or ask for help. But an animal—other than just enduring its karmic experiences—doesn't have the simplest ability to protect itself. Wild animals live in fear of having their lives taken by human and nonhuman enemies and other circumstances. Every mouthful of food or drink is consumed in fear. There is never a moment of complete harmony or peace.

Animals living with human beings go through their own particular suffering. Apart from the few that have a semblance of a good life, most animals living with human beings are consumed for their meat, used for their skins and bones, or enslaved as farm animals or beasts of burden. We inflict enormous pain on animals—piercing their noses, beating them, putting them to work. Burdened with heavy loads to the point of complete collapse, they are beaten to work harder no matter how hot or cold the climate, no matter how difficult the task. It is essential to look at the intense fear and pain that animals go through for something as inconsequential as a piece of meat on our plate, the leather we use, or any of the other things for which animals give their lives.

If you've ever been to a slaughterhouse, you have a very clear idea of an animal's suffering. It would be simpler to think about taking life if you had to look at close range into the eyes of an animal that didn't want to die. No matter how foolish that life form may seem, how incapable of generating awareness or enlightenment, no matter what other reasons we might come up with— when you look into the eyes of an animal who doesn't want to die, who is standing next in line to the one being slaughtered in front of its eyes, at that moment you can truly understand the suffering and fear of the animal realm.

Contemplation

Look carefully at the animal realm beyond your small poodle or cat and see it for what it truly is. In the animal realm—which is a far better existence than the hell and hungry ghost realms—the suffering is intense. Reflect on all the sentient beings suffering like this at this moment. As you and I sit here thinking about their suffering, sentient beings are experiencing the fruition of their karma in each of these realms. If you still feel you have lots of time left to practice, reflect on the intense pain that could become a personal experience based on karma.

To help us appreciate the difficulties of the lower realms and the preciousness of this moment, Terdag Lingpa gave several examples. First, imagine taking your finger and putting it into a flame. In the intensity of that brief moment of burning when you would yell out in pain, see if you can rest in uncontrived mind. Then reflect on the intense heat and burning in the hell realms and on the beings there, who can do little about their state of mind because of the intensity of their pain.

Imagine going out and sitting naked for a while in the cold. When you come inside with your teeth chattering, see if your mind can rest in its uncontrived nature. Think about the sentient beings experiencing a million times more pain and suffering in the cold hells at this very moment.

Or, while sitting in meditation, allow a small insect to bite you. See how even a flea bite shifts your concentration to the pain of that experience. Then think of the constant and intense suffering of the animal realm. Think of how little opportunity these millions of beings have to develop self-awareness or to benefit others, and reflect on the positive circumstances of your own life.

Contemplation

To contemplate the suffering of the three lower realms, devote at least one full day to each of them. For one day, contemplate the intense hunger and thirst of the hungry ghost realm; the inconceivable heat, cold, and pain of the eighteen hell realms; the ignorance, enslavement, and fear of the animal realm, and so on. This isn't a cursory analysis. Reflect deeply on examples and your own personal experiences to really understand the meaning of the suffering of sentient being in the three lower realms.

In this moment, our circumstances are so favorable that—other than the invisible influence of some concept—there's no reason why this mind cannot recognize and rest in its fundamental nature. As you are free from the lower realms, allow yourself to develop genuine tolerance for the little distractions in your mind. This brings us to the three higher realms.

The Three Higher Realms

THE THREE HIGHER REALMS are referred to as the god (*deva*) realm, the jealous god (*asura*) realm, and the human realm. They are higher in the sense that—compared with the lower realms—there is less suffering, the suffering is less intense, and the suffering is mingled with joy and happiness.

These realms are based on what is called ordinary positive karma. Having accumulated positive karma, we're born into a higher realm; we are not, however, free from cyclic existence. Why? Karma is still continuously being created in these realms, and there is a backlog of negative karma that has yet to ripen. When these two factors come together, they may result in our reverting back to the lower realms. We are still on the wheel of cyclic existence, which continues to transfer the consciousness from one realm to the next. So the higher realms do not provide a foundation for ultimate happiness or the exhaustion of suffering.

The Human Realm
The human-realm experiences of suffering are birth, old age, sickness, and death. The experience of birth is a relatively mild

form of suffering compared to the sufferings of the lower realms. Nevertheless, a baby experiences intense fear during birth, which is explained as a great fear of the unknown. And then there is sickness, old age, and death. The whole process of living in this world—with its moments of happiness and harmony—has an undercurrent of impermanence and change, hope and fear. We may spend a lifetime doing something with very little to show for it in terms of genuine essence or usefulness. And—if we don't die young—we will live to experience sickness and old age.

⑤ *Contemplation*

When we enter old age, this lifetime comes to an end. Physically we are no longer able to create life. The body bends, the skin dries up, our face becomes full of wrinkles, and our hair turns white. All of our senses weaken and wane so we can't enjoy the things we want to enjoy. Sitting is uncomfortable, walking is uncomfortable, living is uncomfortable. Our speech stammers and the mind isn't clear or coherent. Everything we've taken to be solid is completely groundless; everything we want to hold on to dissolves and disappears. We need to contemplate these human experiences.

In the human realm, along with every happiness suffering arises. No one born into samsara is free from this suffering, and meanwhile the creation of karma continues. Finally, no matter how worthy or unworthy we are, no matter what kind of authority we have or don't have or how good or bad our life has been, all lives end in death. Our circumstances don't matter at the moment of death. The only thing that matters is the karma we've created in this life.

At the moment, we may be healthy and all of our circumstances may be favorable. We may ignore the fact of suffering and forget about old age, sickness, and death—until unfortunate circumstances strike. Then we can really understand the pain and fear that arise with the decaying or destruction of the body. When—unfortunately or in some cases fortunately—we're given an indication of a life-threatening disease, the mind becomes more grounded in the preciousness of each moment and each day.

Within a small circle of people, things may seem to stay the same with the passing years. When we relate to a larger circle, human suffering is more apparent. In my case, for example, not a day goes by that I don't hear of someone who is dying. Of course, countless beings are dying all the time, but I'm speaking of acquaintances. Whether I am at home or traveling, whenever the telephone rings a part of my mind wonders, "OK, who has died now? Who has just learned they have two or three months to live?" Sickness, old age, and death can strike at any moment. The question is, What do I do now, now that I've been told I have two or three months to live?

The God Realm

The god realm is related to complete joyfulness. There is a sense that all of our positive conditions have come together—which does not mean we're free from cyclic existence. Along with joy comes an immense carelessness about the positive circumstances we've attained, and there is no awareness of relating to suffering at all. Only a mind capable of knowing suffering and the cause of suffering as well as happiness and the cause of happiness can develop the wisdom of discernment. This wisdom is completely lacking in the god realm. For this reason the human realm is said to be superior to the god realm: the human mind understands suffering.

Because the gods' personal experience of joy does not allow for reflection on suffering, the cause of suffering, or the exhaustion of their good karma, the god realm is said to be worse than a hell realm in many ways. In hell realms, negative karma is exhausted; but in god realms, *good* karma is exhausted, which gives rise to nonawareness and the creation of negative karma. When that negative karma combines with any residual negative karma that has yet to ripen, it takes this consciousness to the depths of the lower realms.

It is said that even the god realm, although a very high realm—and realm of Indra, king of gods—must be carefully understood. Due to the force of the karma, even one who reigns over the god realm as "king of devas" falls back into cyclic existence when the god-realm karma is exhausted. Then, through the residual effects of negative karma, one is reborn in the lower realms.

The gods in the various god realms suffer from exhaustion of all good karma through spending eons in a stupor of self-indulgence. The greatest suffering for god-realm beings is the suffering of change and fall. When the good karma that caused one's god-realm birth is exhausted, the intense suffering of change and fall occurs and the god faces the time of death. Realizing that one has wasted millions of years causes intense and immeasurably painful regret. Because of being a god, one knows one will be born in a realm full of suffering, and this gives rise to extreme fear and dread. Birth in the upper realms—even with their temporary pleasures—is the foundation for creating negative karma. To aspire to be born in such realms indicates a lack of awareness and no understanding of the true nature of freedom.

The Jealous God Realm

In the jealous god realm, sometimes known as the demigod realm, there is an intense preoccupation with the god realms. In fact, these two upper realms come together in several ways: They both create karma, the ground on which their karma ripens is the same, and they both inflict warfare on one another. In general, the jealous gods experience constant jealousy and hatred. Unable to bear the happiness of others, they spend most of their time expressing their jealousy and hatred in the form of killing, warfare, and destruction of one another—which eventually leads to rebirth in the Reviving Hell. Since the main activity in this realm is inflicting harm, karma is created.

The creation of karma continues in the three upper realms. The hopes and fears of human beings create karmic seeds of unhappiness, and the hopes and fears of gods and jealous gods also create karma—even more intense in terms of display.

Each of the six realms should be understood in terms of its *predominant* suffering, although all kinds of suffering can be felt in each realm. Human beings, for example, may experience intense heat, cold, hunger, thirst and have hell-realm and hungry ghost–realm experiences—nevertheless, our predominant sufferings are birth, sickness, old age, and death. Hell-realm beings may experience hunger, thirst, and other kinds of pain, but their main sufferings are heat and cold. And hungry ghosts may suffer from heat and cold, jealousy, hatred, and fear, but their predominant suffering is hunger and thirst. Understanding this diversity of suffering is the ground of compassion.

Contemplation

Contemplate the predominant sufferings of each of the six realms. Try to make your mind vast enough to appreciate the diversity of pain and confusion of these sentient beings. If you can do this for each of the realms, good. If you can't, simply allow your mind to go beyond personal unhappiness and suffering to appreciate for a moment the vast confusion and pain of others. This is the ground in which the seed of genuine selfless compassion can be sown.

I 2

The Six Realms: Not Solid—
and Not to Be Taken Lightly

CONTEMPLATING THE SIX REALMS is not just about seeing
the diverse experiences of sentient beings. It is also about letting go of the intense arrogance that thinks the world begins and
ends with "me." By not only creating a favorable karmic ground
for ourselves but also appreciating the suffering of others, we
begin to generate selfless generosity and compassion without bias.
To appreciate that *sameness*, we contemplate the six realms.

The modern world, East and West, tends to solidify the six
realms and their suffering too much. We may think, "I got angry,
I have such aggression, now I'm sure to go to the hell realm"—
and give up on the reasoning behind this. The point is not that we
all go the hell realms for a million years. Is it? The point is to understand that suffering will exist as long as grasping and karmic
patterns exist. Failing to understand our true nature, we revert
again and again to the seeming reality of appearances. By solidifying appearances, we make our creations seem real.

The same grasping and elaborating of perceptions happens in
all the realms. The six realms are created from one moment of distracted grasping, which creates karma, which comes to fruition

as a particular environment—with the emotions, perceptions, and formations of a particular kind of experience. Therefore, the nature of all realms is illusory: every realm is a dream state, with the same fundamental essence as our own.

So the solidity or reality of the six realms is entirely up to us. The most fundamental and true Buddhist view sees the six realms to be no more real than a dream. Reality runs parallel with our grasping at the solidity of appearances—the solidity of sounds, tastes, feelings, thoughts, concepts, and so on. It's entirely up to us how much "reality" we bring to whatever we perceive at this moment. The six realms are just that real; the hell realm is just that real. When we genuinely let go of grasping at each and every concept—even the tiniest concept, even the most subtle grasping—we realize that the core essence of reality is based on the grasping mind itself. When the grasping mind can let go and remain within its true nature, there isn't any such thing as samsara, nirvana, six realms, or sentient beings. At that point everything dissolves into the fundamental ground of awareness. This is the view from the very beginning.

Contemplation

One way to realize your own ground potential is to let go of grasping at the solidity of your perceptions. But how does this ultimate view of true nature compare with your own ability? At this point, your potential may still be stuck in the relative reality of distinguishing between samsara and nirvana. If that sense of separation is still there, you are still solidifying your perceptions—sights, sounds, thoughts, and so on. It's essential to see every appearance in the same way, as having the same consistency and same reality. This is another way to contemplate the reality of the six realms.

The main thing to know about the six realms is that they should not be solidified. They should not be seen as solid states of existence in which we're trapped in inexhaustible suffering. This view can lead to a state of fear. And while fearing the six realms is not a problem from the point of view of practice, ultimately it is not necessary.

On the other hand, we cannot take the suffering of the six realms lightly. If Tibetan practitioners have a serious quarrel among themselves, one might say, "If I can get my point across, I'm not afraid to go to vajra hell"—which is the lowest depth of the lowest hell. Saying this casually is a clear indication of not understanding the tremendous suffering and confusion of samsara. If understood as a state of torment, the hell realms do exist.

We are talking about good, compassionate, responsible minds that shift from awareness in a moment of self-indulgence. As a result of that single karma, we could wander endlessly in a specific environment of suffering. From that perspective, when we talk about a million years burning in fire or boiling in molten lava, we're really talking about a million years lost in ignorance—through a single moment of not understanding our innate essence. Greater than the suffering of the six realms is the complete waste of our time, energy, and abilities, in that we're unable to help ourselves or anyone else.

From that perspective, we cannot take the six realms and their relative sufferings lightly. We enter into the realms when our mind shifts away from the ground of awareness and begins to churn out negative karmas. At that point, hell realms and all the rest are possible. More important is the awareness we bring to this very moment. In this moment, we need not create suffering if we don't want to—which brings us to the next reminder, karma.

Contemplation

A mind that wastes even a moment indulging in hesitation and nonawareness is simply unaware of the pain and suffering of others—and therefore incapable of generating genuine compassion. To be free from that ignorance, we must contemplate the suffering of the six realms and truly value this present moment. Now is the time to develop the ground of positive karma. Even if it's not possible to save or benefit billions of beings, we can at least do that.

PART FOUR

Fourth Thought: Karma

When the time comes for even a king to depart,
Neither his riches nor loved ones, relatives, and friends will
* follow.*
Wherever beings abide, wherever they go,
Karma alone follows them like a shadow.

The three realms blaze with the sufferings of old age and
* sickness,*
And there is no protector from the raging flames of death.
Born into cyclic existence, beings dwell continually in
* ignorance,*
Circling like bees trapped in a jar.

We all know that everyone wants happiness just as much as we do and that no one wants to suffer any more than we do. This understanding of our common ground is the basis of meditation practice and meditation in action. Gentleness, kindness, and unbiased compassion for all sentient beings are necessary simply because all sentient beings want happiness just as much as we do. But simply wanting it won't make it happen. For that we must truly understand karma, the law of cause and effect.

1 3

The Law of Karma

BUDDHISM IS A NONTHEISTIC philosophy. We do not believe in a creator but in the causes and conditions that create certain circumstances that then come to fruition. This is called karma. It has nothing to do with judgment; there is no one keeping track of our karma and sending us up above or down below. Karma is simply the *wholeness* of a cause, or first action, and its effect, or fruition, which then becomes another cause. In fact, one karmic cause can have many fruitions, all of which can cause thousands more creations. Just as a handful of seed can ripen into a field full of grain, a small amount of karma can generate limitless effects.

Every conditioned phenomenon—human beings, the environment, and so on—is the effect of individual or collective karma manifesting in completely diverse ways. For example, we can talk about "first karma," the reverberation of one karma striking or coming together with another. One karmic moment can immediately split into the ten directions and three times— and each of those ten directions can again explode into ten more directions. The expansion and multiplicity of karma is said to be like a billion universes colliding with another billion universes. This is the fruition aspect of karma, which we will talk about in more detail later.

So karma does not just refer to big blocks of anger, ignorance, or negative emotions; it can be subtle. A flicker of movement, a simple nod of the head to indicate a feeling, a subtle movement of the eyes can establish karmic cause and eventual fruition. The textures of our sense perceptions—sights, sounds, smells, touch, tastes, and thoughts—create hundreds of karmic causes at every moment. The moment we shift from our fundamental ground, we create a karmic cause that produces some effect—for better or worse.

Contemplation

Our entanglement with sensory display leads to actions that create karma. Reflect on the fact that, in this precious and pure moment, all attachment and aggression could completely disintegrate; nevertheless, we detour again and again into the display of the senses. The samsaric cycle continues, and all our hard work becomes meaningless and lacking in benefit or fruition. Suffering is meeting every fresh moment absolutely capable of transforming it and not taking the opportunity to do so. What could be sadder than that?

Karma can be intentional or unintentional. The actions we're aware of and those we're not aware of—which are most of our actions—produce karmic effects for ourselves and others. To understand how this works, we need to watch ourselves in action and understand our potential for immensely diverse karmic production, good and bad.

We can also talk about collective karma. The karma of many sentient beings bringing a lack of awareness to their actions can lead to the collective fruition of war, famine, and diseases that are experienced by everyone. All the pain and suffering in samsara are the result of individual or collective karmic creation.

As individuals or groups—on a tribal or national level, or just within samsara as a whole—we are all creating karma and being affected by the karma created by others. Similarly, others are creating karma and being affected by the karma we create. There is always this interchange of karma. At the same time, karma can be changed; karma is exhaustible and impermanent.

14

Creating Positive and Negative Karma

THE SIMPLEST WAY to understand good and bad karma is this: virtuous actions produce virtuous results and negative actions produce negative results. Good karma produces a good fruition such as happiness, and bad karma comes to fruition as suffering.

The fundamental discipline of Buddhism is to abandon unvirtuous actions and cultivate virtuous action. To know which actions to abandon, we need to know what unvirtuous actions are. In general, they are any actions arising out of nonawareness and self-clinging. In particular, they are actions contaminated by the three root poisons: aggression, attachment, and ignorance—which together with pride and jealousy are known as the five root poisons. When any of these root poisons creep into the actions of our body, speech, and mind—whether we're aware of it or not—those actions are unvirtuous.

When we see how much pain and suffering our self-clinging causes, we may feel a sense of guilt, regret, or blame. It's important to look at this carefully. To truly understand karma, the words *guilt*, *regret*, and *blame* aren't necessary; we need only know its cause. The root cause of karma is ignorance—and acting out of ignorance was not our intention. If we intended to be ignorant and generate suffering, there might be something to blame or re-gret. But exactly whom are we going to burn at the stake? That's something to contemplate! We have to understand the *totality* of samsara. We can talk about how it all comes down to ignorance and self-grasping with all its habitual tendencies, but what good comes from this unfortunate point? The real point is to appreciate our inherent awareness and develop our human potential.

Contemplation

Awareness is the ground of good karma and the fruition of happiness. Seeing your negative tendencies and ignorance should only cause you to strengthen that positive ground. Your good human qualities far outweigh and are far superior to any negative circumstances. There is also the tremendous potential inherent in external circumstances. Given this pos-itive ground, you could completely liberate all confusion and ignorance this very moment. This is the essential way for a meditator to train the mind.

If we recognize suffering and don't do anything to change it, we only succumb further. Instead of overcoming the problem with wisdom and compassion, we keep coming back to the prob-lem. This is precisely what is meant by habitual patterns. This is the ignorance we've been stuck in all along—and the root cause of suffering. To cut this root, we need discipline and an under-standing of how to create *good* karma, if only from the point of view of not harming others.

Out of compassion for sentient beings, we have a responsibil-ity to bring more awareness to our relationship with the world. Each moment of the day, we perform limitless actions deeply em-bedded with selfishness, grasping, aggression, or ignorance. Be-cause they are too numerous to count, they're summed up as ten unvirtuous actions.

15

The Ten Unvirtuous Actions

THERE ARE TEN ACTIONS that we must become completely aware of and completely abandon in our lives. Bringing them to mind often reminds me of monastics about to take ordination. When we first hear the vows, we're so enthusiastic and confident that we will never commit any of the root downfalls. After all, none of us goes around stealing, or killing, or telling lies. But after taking the vows and observing ourselves more carefully, we find there's hardly any action that doesn't hurt someone or cause some kind of harm. Because of that awareness, we're able to train ourselves to become better.

Sometimes people get very rigid and tense trying to be good, disciplined, and ethical. Tension can also arise when we become more aware of the immense amount of destruction—seen and unseen, intentional and unintentional—that our mere physical existence causes. From a Buddhist point of view, however, this is what it means to be born in samsara, and this is why we need to attain freedom from samsara.

The actions we must completely abandon are divided into three unvirtuous actions of body, four unvirtuous actions of speech, and three unvirtuous actions of mind.

The Three Unvirtuous Actions of Body: Killing, Stealing, and Sexual Misconduct

KILLING can be understood in many ways. We create subtle killing karma every moment of our lives. Nevertheless, killing has to combine with some degree of intent. For an action to fully arise as the karma of killing, we must have the intention to kill and then perform the act. This means we intend to kill, we plan the act, and we make no mistake about whom we're killing. To kill even a small insect, for example, we must identify the insect, have the intention to kill it, and act upon that. To perform the act of killing completely, we must act with aggression. This is what is known as killing. In Tibetan, killing also implies that, until the sentient being is completely dead, the intention to kill is continuous.

The main thing here is the heaviness of the karma of killing. The karma of some killing activities may be less intense due to the absence of a strong intention or desire to kill, the absence of an intended being, or the absence of aggression—although as long as the act is completed, there is aggression. We need to understand killing from all these perspectives and not necessarily feel that we're going to the hell realms because of unintentionally taking life. Killing needs to be properly understood.

STEALING, the second unvirtuous action of body, means taking something that doesn't belong to us. Whatever means we use— rank, physical strength, authority, verbal skills, flattery, threats, or other actions or tricks—to take what does not belong to us or is not willingly given to us is stealing. Now, again most of us don't think we go about stealing things, but stealing is the one thing we may do more often than anything else. Even the intent or wish— through envy or jealousy—to have something that doesn't belong to us can be seen as stealing. So contemplate carefully what it means to take what doesn't belong to you.

SEXUAL MISCONDUCT, the third unvirtuous action of body, refers to the pain or harm we inflict on another—our partner or anyone else—for the fulfillment of our own wishes. Our intention and physical actions express only self-indulgence. We are not at all sensitive to the feelings, nature, or state of mind of the other person. Not being aware of another's needs while continuing to fulfill our own is said to be sexual misconduct. To take advantage of someone who is unwilling or reluctant, to hurt someone's feelings, or to inflict harm in any way—these things need to be seen as sexual misconduct. These three unvirtuous actions of the body need to be carefully understood.

The Four Unvirtuous Actions of Speech: Lying, Slander, Harsh Speech, and Idle Chatter

LYING means not speaking the truth. The intention is to fool or deceive someone or to intentionally give misinformation. For our own personal gain, we knowingly say something that's not true. The act of lying is complete when the intention to deceive completely convinces another that what we are saying is true when in fact it's not. And lying is not only linked with speech. A sign given through bodily actions could also be a lie. If we don't want to answer a question, we might shrug our shoulders and walk away. So physical actions can also support deception.

People often ask if it would be better to lie in order to help someone than to tell the truth and harm the person. If we think about this carefully, we'll see that the definition of lying talks about the intention to deceive someone for personal gain. If a lie is not for our own benefit, it doesn't fully meet the definition of the unvirtuous act of lying. Of course, there is some karmic negativity with any act of lying, and that karma will come to fruition for us. But if that lie benefits someone else, it is far more virtuous than telling the truth.

SLANDER, or sowing discord through speech, is the second unvirtuous act of speech. It's an unvirtuous action because we want to sow the seed of discord for our own benefit. Between two people or two groups, for example, we use speech to create a sense of suspicion that results in discord. The impact of sowing discord through speech can vary. When the act comes to fruition, the karma is complete. The karma may be lessened if the act does not come to completion. If others are not convinced of what we say, for example, the karma is not complete. So we need to understand the various aspects of this slander.

HARSH SPEECH is the third unvirtuous act of speech. This is speech with the intention to harm. We might say something negative or critical to hurt someone's feelings. If our criticism is heard, it destroys that person's peace of mind, which is said to be the complete action of harsh speech.

IDLE CHATTER or gossip is the fourth unvirtuous action of speech. Idle chatter means speaking on any topic in a way that supports nonawareness in ourselves or others. It is speech that distracts the mind, causing it to wander from the fundamental ground and grasp at various forms of entertainment. Creating such a ground of nonawareness is gossip or idle chatter. Terdag Lingpa refers to idle chatter as the main reason for the creation of karma. If we examine carefully, we'll see that most of our speech that is *not* slander, harsh speech, or lies falls into the category of idle chatter or gossip.

Idle chatter is the action on which we waste the most time. So it is particularly harmful since it wastes this precious human existence and accomplishes absolutely no benefit for anyone.

🌀 *Contemplation*

The best way to benefit another person is through selflessness. Remember that it's not about the constant creation of
good karma; it's about maintaining the discipline and karma
of genuine selflessness. A seemingly unvirtuous action can
arise as a virtuous action if the intention is selfless. This is
how we should look at things.

The Three Unvirtuous Actions of Mind: Covetousness, Wishing Harm on Others, and Wrong View

COVETOUSNESS means seeing and wanting for ourselves the
possessions of others—homes, families, wealth, rank, knowledge, wisdom, abilities, beauty, power, and other desirable qualities. Rather than strengthening our own positive qualities, we
reflect on what we do not have, which gives rise to jealousy, depression, or disappointment in ourselves. Covetousness is about
poverty mentality. Instead of focusing on strengthening the
ground of our own practices, we give in to feeling sorry for ourselves. This is the negative action of covetousness.

WISHING HARM ON OTHERS, the second unvirtuous action of
mind, means genuinely wanting another sentient being to suffer.
It is our wish that they come to harm, that unfortunate circumstances befall them, or that we ourselves could—through an act
of body, speech, or mind—cause them maximum pain and harm.

WRONG VIEW is the third unvirtuous action of mind. Simply
put, wrong view is not having confidence in cause and effect. This
is the result of not understanding the various experiences of samsaric existence: birth into a samsaric realm, the suffering of sentient beings in samsara, and the value or significance of the Three

Jewels. Where these things are not contemplated and understood, confidence does not arise. This is the ground of wrong view.

Wrong view is not about believing one thing as opposed to another. Wrong view means not allowing truth to arise in the mind—not a Buddhist or non-Buddhist truth, but human truth, the truth of human potential and what this human life can actually create. The real meaning of wrong view is that in spite of understanding this, we don't do anything about it. We understand the potential of this human life and do not put it into practice. Wrong view therefore is about the truth of suffering: the truth is that all sentient beings want happiness but the truth of karma does not allow that happiness to arise.

The point here is to abandon the wrong view of not believing in cause and effect. Having confidence in karma inspires us to be more aware of the actions of our body, speech, and mind. In this way, we don't inflict harm on others and we can actually generate some good, some cause of happiness for ourselves and others. Freedom from wrong view is freedom from carelessness or non-awareness. This includes our unintentional actions—unintentional killing, unintentional lying, unintentionally inflicting harm. While these may not be "fully" unvirtuous actions, they must also be abandoned. We cannot simply say, "Oh, this isn't really killing," and therefore not regret that karma. The point is to relate to our unvirtuous actions and to cultivate their opposites, the ten virtuous actions.

16

The Fruition of Negative Karma

FRUITION CAN BE UNDERSTOOD in various ways. First we can talk about general fruition, which refers to the intention with which karma is generated. We can have high, medium, or low levels of intention, which determine corresponding levels of karmic fruition. The resulting karma if anger arises, for example, is determined by whether the intention is great, medium, or slight. If there was no intention to harm anyone, there is little karmic fruition. If our words, thoughts, or deeds contained a powerful intention to cause harm and resulted in the act of killing, the fruition would be rebirth in the hell realm. With medium intention we would be reborn in the hungry ghost realm, and with little intention in the animal realm. Similarly, our actions could lead to birth in the god, jealous god, or human realm. The kind and degree of suffering depend on the degree of intention.

Contemplation

The distance between this moment—sitting with the assuredness of a meditator reflecting on these sufferings—and actually experiencing the suffering of the lower realms is the distance of a single breath. Between inhaling and exhaling, your breath could be disrupted or lose its life force and death would occur. Your accumulated karma could then lead to such experiences—believe it or not, it's absolutely possible. Reflect therefore on the ground of your experience and really strengthen that ground with awareness. Exert effort to overcome any little problems or obstacles and to transcend any fears or confusion. At this moment, you have the possibility of purifying the ground of negative karma. It's essential to go in that direction.

The fruition of karma depends on its cause. Because of stealing, we might face poverty throughout our life. Sexual misconduct is said to result in argumentative spouses and marital discord in the next lifetime. Because of lying, we could face criticism, false accusations, and treachery throughout our life. Because of sowing discord, we could face disharmony and argument at all times. Harsh speech might result in constantly hearing negative things said about us and being insulted and belittled. Because of gossip, people might not trust what we say; our speech won't inspire trust in their minds and our words will carry no weight. Covetousness could result in none of our hopes being fulfilled and bring about unwanted circumstances and conditions. The intention to harm could come to fruition as a human life filled with fear and constant harm. And wrong view could cause us to succumb to ignorance throughout our life, no matter how much we'd like to free ourselves, and to suffer from deceit and misconceptions.

But the karmic fruition of a particular type of karmic action is not always the same. We can't simply say that all killing leads to the hell realm. Taking life unintentionally or without the motivation of aggression may result in some painful experience or disability in the human realm, for example. We might be very well born and endowed with many good qualities but live a very short life—which is not to say that everyone who lives a short life has killed. People often ask, "Does a short life necessarily mean that someone has killed in a previous life?" The answer is no. There are diverse causes and fruitions of karma.

It may be that we don't experience *any* karmic fruition in this life. Karmic fruition can be experienced immediately or after a few days, months, or even lifetimes. Again, we must understand the diversity of karmic fruition. The karma of killing might become more gross or powerful over time and then in the next lifetime—although we're born in the human realm endowed with all the qualities and potential for a good life—karma comes to fruition as the desire to kill. We might *like* the notion of killing and want to continue killing until it becomes a habitual pattern. So killing might come to fruition as a habitual pattern rather than a short life. Watching people's habitual patterns, we can see the subtle ways in which karma comes to fruition.

On the other hand, we might be completely free from fruition, which arises instead in the environment. As a result of killing, we might be born in a war-torn or violent country, where there's a lack of medicine or food. Stealing could result in a decrease in wealth, health, and other positive circumstances in the land. Sexual misconduct could result in an entire land suffering from various diseases or famine. Lying, harsh speech, or gossip could result in a country where no crops grow—such as a desert where the land is dry and unable to produce grain, water, or happiness—and karmic fruition is experienced as the extreme suffering of all sentient beings. So the karma of killing and other unvirtuous actions can come to fruition as collective karma that ripens in the environment.

Now, one individual's act of killing is not going to result in an entire land facing famine or violence, but the ongoing karma of many sentient beings can lead to the collective fruition of war, famine, and diseases experienced by everyone. So again we can see the diversity of karmic fruition.

17

The Ten Virtuous Actions
and the Fruition of Positive Karma

A T THIS POINt, we can talk about the fruition of positive karma. The ten virtuous actions of body, speech, and mind are the exact opposite of unvirtuous actions, namely, awareness of body, awareness of speech, and awareness of mind. Bringing awareness to all our activities brings karma to the path of practice. To take this as our path, we must (1) recognize our actions of body, speech, and mind; (2) discern between virtuous and unvirtuous actions; and (3) free all our actions from the contamination of ignorance, desire, or attachment.

If we focus too much on the blackness and bleakness of karma, we forget about the brightness of virtue. That should not happen in the mind of the meditator. Positive karma also comes to fruition. Just as negative karma leads to birth in the lower realms, the power of positive karma creates even greater positive fruition. As with negative karma, the fruition of positive karma is connected with motivation. Even a moment of awareness combined with the motivation of compassion toward all sentient beings can result in a vast expanse of good karma that genuinely benefits others. If a moment of unawareness can cause us to succumb to ignorance and cause suffering, a moment of awareness can bring the mind back and cause limitless benefit.

Virtuous actions are also motivated by greater, medium, and lesser motivation. Lesser motivation has to do with giving rise to happiness or benefit for oneself. Medium motivation is able to connect with others to some extent—friends, families, and so on. And the greatest motivation is the vastness of compassion for all sentient beings.

Traditionally, it is said that birth in the upper realms is actually quite easy to attain, simply by leading a decent life. Some texts say that the kinds of lives most of us live almost guarantee birth in the upper realms. Every moment we spend sustaining life is a virtuous action. All the actions of our body, speech, and mind that are not only for our own survival but for the wellbeing of family, community, and human life are virtuous actions—as is the treasuring of our own body and life. There is the fruition of good karma in all of this. With the greater motivation to benefit limitless beings in whatever way possible, simply being alive allows virtuous karma to be limitless. This is the way positive fruition works.

The various kinds of fruition of positive karma are long life, not having enemies or difficulties with anyone adverse to us, hearing praises and other good things said about ourselves, easily developing trust and faith with others, having genuine happiness and peace of mind, and having our hopes and expectations fulfilled. Through our accumulating positive karma, these positive fruitions arise.

Contemplation

Our birth was not merely the fruition of negative karma, but also the realization of the eighteen qualities with which we are now endowed. Just being able to read and understand these profound instructions is the fruition of the virtuous karma we have accumulated—which can therefore be taken further. This virtuous karma also affects the entire environment: a single positive thought can arise as peace in the environment; a single compassionate thought dedicated to sentient beings can arise in innumerable ways as the cause of happiness for limitless beings. Just as the power of negative karma can create unhappiness, the power of virtuous karma can create happy circumstances for sentient beings. We need to understand this.

Earlier we talked about a third motivation that is neither virtuous nor unvirtuous. This neutral motivation is a kind of sleep, stupor, or dullness that gives rise to neutral karma. Any action that doesn't arise from aggression or attachment is neutral: eating without aggression or attachment, walking without aggression or attachment, and so on. Such actions can become beneficial if brought into awareness. Otherwise they are indicative of ignorance, a waste of time, and need to be abandoned.

Awareness is such a simple thing. Joined with the simple act of eating, for example, it brings the awareness of eating. With that awareness we can dedicate the virtue of eating to all beings: "Just as this eating satisfies my hunger, may all sentient beings enjoy the same satisfaction and be free from any unhappiness. May the enjoyment of this food arise as benefit for all beings." In this way, dedicate your actions with any positive thoughts you can generate. In the *Bodhicharyavatara*, Shantideva says that contemplating karma should give rise to a deep awareness that does not leave us even in sleep or dreams. Not constantly distracted by outer manifestations and judgments, we can truly cut through habitual tendencies of grasping and remain in awareness that is as constant as space.

While actions are described as virtuous, unvirtuous, or neutral, we need to understand—through contemplating karma—

that all actions are virtuous when they arise from a virtuous intention. Any action motivated by the benefit of others is a virtuous action. Any action motivated by self-gratification or self-indulgence—no matter how spiritual or ethical it may seem—is still a negative action. The main point is motivation.

Karma continues as long as we create the cause. Without confidence in karma, we may still hope for happiness to fall into our lives from on high. Maybe our practices will dispel suffering and bring about enlightenment without our having to work hard or embody the teachings. Maybe we'll be the exceptional case on whom enlightenment will descend from space. This is like a very thirsty person who, instead of simply drinking the water he or she already has, puts it into a vessel with tea and milk, ties it to the top of a tree, lights a fire beneath it, and waits for it to boil—and meanwhile dies of thirst.

Similarly, we have our teachers and teachings, our meditation cushions and shrines, and the motivation to do something good. But we sit down to meditate with the *hope* that something will happen. The tendency to wait and hope is very theistic and solid. It may not seem as solid as a creator "up there," but a hope or expectation is definitely a creation, which is no different. Understanding this, all of us—on this or any other path—have a responsibility to look honestly at our lives and practice.

18

Karma and Reincarnation

A T THIS POINT, PEOPLE often ask about reincarnation. Reincarnation is just an honorific term for karma. If you have some understanding of cause and effect, reincarnation is very easy to understand and not a big deal. Yes, we do talk about great teachers reincarnating from one life to another; and yes, from that perspective, great masters are able to remember previous lives. But reincarnation must be understood properly. It is not about flashbacks of previous lives, as many people imagine. It's about cause and effect and the karmic ground that we accumulate.

When there are fewer negative emotions and habitual tendencies, the karmic ground is more clear. That clarity continues by virtue of not accumulating negative karma. Bodhisattvas and enlightened teachers are able to have continuous clarity of mind. Because the karma of clarity is continuous, it is easier for clarity to manifest and easier to pick up on. The maturation of clear karma —which arises as clear awareness, or wisdom—occurs much more quickly and is much more connected with the activities of their lives. Ordinary people like us have to deal with a mishmash of virtuous and unvirtuous karma, which takes more time. It's the difference between a clear path and a thorny, bushy path where we must make our way more carefully. Our ordinary reincarnation is all about karma and fruition, which creates more karma, and so on.

⑤ Contemplation

Milarepa taught that if you want to know who you were in your previous life or who you will be in the future, you have only look to this present life. If your life is good and comfortable, endowed with favorable circumstances and qualities, then you will know that you were a virtuous person in your previous life, which was definitely led with some awareness. Similarly, to know what your next life will be like, you have only to look at the kinds of actions, or karma, you are accumulating now. This is the foundation of the next realm or kind of environment into which you'll be born. Examine your life carefully. Contemplate the number of years that you've lived and the kind of karma you've accumulated until now.

No matter how enlightened we may be, no matter how immense our compassion and understanding, if we are born of a father and mother as a human being in this world system, we are subject to karma. Our previous karma may be very clear, but the important thing is the karma we create in this life. It doesn't take long for crystal-clear karma to become muddy. That's always a possibility. Clarity of karma can manifest in varying degrees in the reincarnations of teachers and their activities—which is an honorific term for a teacher's karma. The awareness that must be maintained for clarity of karma to continue is the same for all sentient beings.

Purification of Body, Speech, and Mind

PRACTICALLY SPEAKING, it is very difficult—but essential—to bring the mind back to awareness and free ourselves from the habitual patterns that create karma. The path of training the mind therefore introduces various practices

PURIFICATION OF BODY includes practices such as sitting meditation, circumambulation and prostrations, which physically bring the mind back to awareness and free the body from creating negative karma. Such "physical" spiritual practices enable us to develop and maintain awareness and to transform habitual tendencies of the body so that instead of harming others, our physical actions become beneficial.

PURIFICATION OF SPEECH includes practices such as the recitation of praises, supplications, prayers, or mantras. These skillful means transform speech by overcoming habitual patterns and negative tendencies. Mantra practice, for example, uses the same essential power of speech to create the ground of more virtuous karma. If we are unable to let go of harmful speech—gossip, idle chatter, and all speech that creates negative karma—we can rely on these practices to transform our speech into something compassionate and beneficial for all sentient beings.

PURIFICATION OF MIND includes skillful means such as devotion, confidence, faith, revulsion for samsara, the Four Thoughts That Transform the Mind, and the generation of loving-kindness and compassion for sentient beings through *tonglen*. Such practices transform the mind so that it generates virtuous instead of unvirtuous actions. Without such supports, mind will continue thinking in its habitual ways and give rise to all the same thoughts. To bring the mind back to awareness, we must rely on skillful supports—contemplation, visualization, recitation, or meditation—that are free from self-grasping. It is essential to understand the influence of mind on our words and deeds. When the mind is trained, it immediately brings awareness to the body, to speech, and to our thoughts. In this way, we create a more favorable ground less contaminated with the three root poisons.

The main thing to understand from contemplating karma is that all actions have a motivation and that motivation needs to be examined. For this we must turn inward and develop awareness of body, speech, and mind. Then we will not only aspire to selfless compassion and generosity, we will actually be able to put them into practice. Our contemplation should lead to the discipline of not creating harmful karma. As much as possible, no action of our body, speech, or mind should arise from nonawareness or distraction. No one needs the karma of harming others due to a momentary lack of awareness, when deep down in our hearts, our intention is to help all sentient beings.

20

The Fruition of Contemplating
the Four Reminders

THE FRUITION OF CONTEMPLATING the Four Reminders is known as letting go of the three graspings and giving rise to the three exertions. We could call them the three types of letting-go and the three accomplishments. We won't have any benefit from our practices—no matter how much we meditate, visualize, recite mantras, or do any spiritual practice—until we generate the three letting gos and the three accomplishments.

FIRST IS LETTING GO OF GRASPING AT OUR VARIOUS AC-
TIVITIES AND ATTACHMENTS. This is the fruition of contemplating the preciousness and impermanence of human life. As a result, we understand the importance of creating the ground for rebirth in the three higher realms—by which we mean specifically a favorable human existence where we might meet with even better circumstances than we enjoy now.

SECOND IS LETTING GO OF ATTACHMENT TO THE EXTREMES
OF SAMSARA. This is the fruition of contemplating samsaric suffering and karma. With this comes the understanding that even

birth in the upper realms is not a complete fruition. We then have a deeper understanding of liberation, or enlightenment, which allows us to really transform our mind.

At this point, we may run into a problem with poverty mentality, or what we could call weakened heart. Becoming more aware of our habitual patterns and seeing how we continue to give in to ignorance, we may struggle with a sense of inadequacy. In the chaos and confusion of ordinary life, we may not notice this problem. Given the time and space to reflect, however, we actually come into contact with an enormous amount of goodness. Poverty mentality is feeling that we cannot generate this goodness in ourselves. This leads us to believe in a very ordinary and inadequate self—with all kinds of discursive thoughts that undermine our confidence in enlightenment.

Without confidence, instead of exerting genuine effort and urgency in our practices, we tend to lessen our hope in fruition. Instead of strengthening "this," we try to make "that" easier. If we make the fruition easier, we won't have to work so hard or transcend anything at all. Instead of enlightenment, we settle for something else.

We Tibetans are very good at this. Hardly anyone talks about enlightenment these days. At most we say, "May I again be born as a human being, *but* with a better teacher, better conditions, in a better place, and not so poor." This is not a particularly Tibetan or Buddhist problem; it's *our* problem. In the beginning, we have maximum enthusiasm, but talk to those who've been Buddhists for twenty or thirty years. You will find that "enlightenment" is something said in passing. We may not even think about the next life; instead we think, "May I be able to die without fear or regret"—or, even worse, "May I be able to hang on until the next retreat." To let go of the poverty mentality that can aspire only to be born again as a human being, contemplate the sufferings of samsara and karma.

Contemplation

It is important not to enter this path with half-hearted intentions or wrong motivation. Remember that poverty mentality is a key to misunderstanding, which opens up all kinds of unnecessary fears and anxieties. As you struggle with these unnecessary concepts, remember too that they will come up again and again in your life. It's important to understand this process from the very beginning. Then years from now when these tendencies arise, you can say to yourself, "Oh, yes, this is to be expected, this is what happens." This recollection will help overcome the impact of neurotic tendencies and allow them to dissolve. Remembering this, generate strong confidence and honesty in your practice.

THIRD IS LETTING GO OF GRASPING AT A SELF. This is the fruition of contemplating all of the Four Reminders. Grasping at a self includes grasping at our own liberation. In the beginning, of course, our main aspiration is "May I be able to attain enlightenment," or "May I be able to really benefit all sentient beings." We're highly motivated by these aspirations, but if we're honest about it there's always that little hope of keeping a safe spot for ourselves. This brings a certain amount of deceit into our lives: we talk about benefiting all sentient beings when in fact we're aiming for individual liberation. As our understanding of the Buddhist view deepens, we can see the error in such statements. As a result, we develop the mahayana understanding of true love and compassion.

Contemplation

If you could have one human life—forget about many lifetimes, just one human life—grounded in *sanity*, it would be harmonious and positive. It would generate goodness for yourself and others and be free from ignorance, selfishness, anger, attachment, greed, confusion, and chaos. Ask yourself if you are spending your life grasping at an individual self, which generates separation, judgments, and conflict with others. Are you so stuck on your own happiness—hoping to maintain it and fearing you cannot—that when a genuine taste of happiness *does* arise it is always tainted with hope and fear? Contemplate the fruition of grasping at illusions and ask yourself if that's what you want.

Selflessness in the Beginning,
Middle, and End

AT PRESENT, we are working with selfish reasoning—self-ish in the sense that, intentionally or unintentionally, "I" takes precedence. Selfishness arises as attachment to individual liberation. Now, it is true that prior to benefiting sentient beings, we have to work with the ground of self-liberation. Nevertheless, even if the mind isn't courageous enough to understand this, it is *selflessness* that brings about enlightenment. Selflessness means letting go of self in the beginning, letting go in the middle, and letting go in the end.

When we are too self-focused, we think it's all about "me:" me and the hell realms, me and my ambition, me and sentient beings, me and my enlightenment. But, in fact, we are deeply affected by the karma of other sentient beings. Without sentient beings, there's no such thing as enlightenment. The good karma, good wishes, and tonglen of others are partly responsible for your reading this today. There is also the fact of Shakyamuni Buddha turning the wheel of Dharma, and the Sangha working very hard to create the right conditions for everyone to practice. And there is your own hard work, merit, compassion, and kindness. So it's a combined effort of everyone's karma working together.

Interdependence is about the karmic patterns of a whole vast world system—and not just about *my* life and suffering, *my* wisdom and views, *my* body, mind, and thoughts. This kind of thinking shows a mistaken belief in a solid self, which we know cannot be established. So how can we be filled with pride and arrogance in the midst of this vast karmic creation? Grasping at a self that is so tiny compared with the vastness of the universe is a very ignorant thing to do—yet when you put down this book, you will still think that "I" put it down.

Appreciation of collective karma creates a greater sense of responsibility to generate the true fruition, which requires an enormous number of positive conditions. We ignore this when we think only of our own achievements. This egoistic approach must be checked. Otherwise the day will come when we realize that others know more than we do, and we will be very upset: "It was I who was going to save all sentient beings, and now I'm being shown the path by others!" This is a very uncomfortable feeling. Trying to attain selflessness by preserving a self to benefit others is not only illogical, it is deceptive. It's just another example of ignorance trying to prove its existence and protect its territory.

All practices and instructions are based on knowing which antidote to apply to obstacles. An obstacle is any tendency of conceptual mind that does not allow the pure intention and meaning of Dharma to arise. The most effective antidote for such obstacles is to contemplate the Four Reminders and generate genuine compassion.

The antidote to *any* egoism is to rejoice in the achievements and merit of others. This includes all the buddhas and bodhisattvas whose blessings and compassion made it possible for us to realize the ground of awareness. Rejoicing in the achievements of others can also alleviate suffering. The karma of suffering is lessened when we appreciate all the positive thoughts being generated toward us by others. When gratitude to others is understood, it becomes even more important to practice sincerely and honestly.

Contemplation

To cut through selfishness, contemplate the Four Reminders and generate the mahayana principle of bodhichitta. Generating the genuine compassion of loving-kindness dispels the ignorance that grasps at individual liberation. Contemplating the Four Reminders and the selflessness arising from bodhichitta forms the foundation of right view. This is the view we need to take into meditation so that our meditation is not fabricated or conceptual. To generate enlightened mind, it is essential to spend time studying and contemplating these things.

PART FIVE

Refuge

Entering the Gateway

THIS PRECIOUS HUMAN LIFE is an opportunity to enter the gateway of liberation. Entering the gateway refers particularly to taking refuge in the Three Jewels of Buddha, Dharma, and Sangha. Through the gateway of refuge, we enter into the vastness and profundity of the Buddhist teachings. Taking refuge is the most profound commitment to arise from intrinsic mind: it is the commitment to realize absolute truth. The fruition of enlightenment is based on this commitment. Because of it, we are able to maintain awareness of body, speech, and mind and to generate a genuine ability to benefit sentient beings.

There are three basic motivations for taking refuge, which simply means seeking protection or guidance. In the beginning, we take refuge to escape from the suffering of the three lower realms. Then, we come to desire liberation from the suffering of samsara altogether—still, however, from the point of view of self-liberation. The third and highest motivation is to genuinely dispel all stains of ignorance so that all sentient beings may attain freedom from suffering.

A BEGINNER'S MOTIVATION is simply to be free from the pain and suffering of the three lower realms. Whether or not we put it in so many words, fear of karmic fruition and a desire to be free from suffering, confusion, and immediate difficulties—which means freedom from the three lower realms—is the initial motivation of our actions and practice.

Our hearts have been truly shaken by the enormous amount of karma we create. We know that whatever we do affects ourselves and others and that this impact isn't temporary but generates enormous continuity and growth. We have some sense of how collective karma and individual karma are interrelated: how a single individual can impact a whole community and how the collective karma of tribes, countries, and so on can shape our individual karma. Even if we don't believe in the realms, we want to be free from this suffering. And we have *some* understanding of the fundamental truth of emptiness, which is innate and doesn't depend on the path of practice alone. We may do our best not to think about these things, but still our understanding grows, especially if we're walking on the path of practice. With this understanding, we take refuge.

At this point, some people ask if we need to believe in reincarnation to take refuge. The answer is no, but it's absolutely necessary to believe in cause and effect. Otherwise, it would be very difficult to understand the importance of being careful with our actions. We wouldn't understand the need to let go of grasping, jealousy, hatred, or anger or to refrain from harming others—and this karma would continue to create suffering. When we see this, a certain embarrassment should arise, and a sense of responsibility and urgency, a sense of "What can I do?"

Taking refuge with that sense of urgency and enormous responsibility, we can sincerely say, "May I strengthen my commitment to develop awareness of body, speech, and mind. May the karma that constantly creates fruition actually generate some good. Through my mindfulness and awareness, may every act be an act of kindness and awareness. If this is not possible, may I at least create some happiness—and at the very least not harm others."

When we speak about beginner's motivation, we are not saying that everyone should *really* have mahayana motivation. Let's say you've just gotten divorced, and to get over your ex-husband, you want to take refuge. You want to dedicate your life to renunciation and practice—until you meet the next person. This kind of motivation is also all right. It's a beginning. Beginner's mind doesn't mean you've burned your bridges; you're actually making a start. And it would be fair to say that there will be gradual progress in working with and deepening your mind. Many of us who have taken refuge may still be practicing for our own personal salvation and freedom from suffering, which is beginner's motivation.

MEDIUM MOTIVATION begins with a similar attitude. Having heard and contemplated the Dharma, we see how ignorance perpetuates the creation of karma. Since the path to liberation is to stop creating karmic causes, we begin to practice with strict discipline. We base our practice on abandoning unvirtuous actions and accumulating virtuous actions. Resting in the essence of meditation, we strengthen that so we can abstain from creating the causes of birth in cyclic existence. We also aspire to attain the state of liberation—but it still only encompasses oneself. We take refuge with this aspiration: "Through the path of practice, may I truly overcome the suffering of samsara in this lifetime." This is called the refuge of devotion, because—in addition to wanting to escape the lower realms—we begin to have devotion to the path of practice. This allows us to attain liberation and freedom from karmic consequences.

Beginning and medium motivation are known as lesser or lower compared to the mahayana, the bodhisattva path. Bodhisattvas are considered superior because their motivation for practice goes beyond personal liberation.

MAHAYANA MOTIVATION includes the liberation of all sentient beings. It has the quality of altruism—but what does this actually mean? Is it enough just to remember sentient beings in our practice? At the beginning of our meditation, we recite, "May all sentient beings attain happiness and the cause of happiness. May they be free from suffering and the cause of suffering." And at the end, we say, "By this merit, may all sentient beings attain omniscience." But are we truly committed to what we say?

We are not really mahayana meditators if we're still holding on to an "I." We may assume we have compassion and a desire to benefit all sentient beings, but nevertheless, whether we recognize it or not, our own contentment, satisfaction, and desires may still be of primary importance. This underlying grasping may undermine our motivation and commitment. Becoming a bodhisattva depends not on vows and initiations but on the maturity and strength of our mind—and our ability not only to talk about including sentient beings but actually to do so.

How do we do this? Sentient beings are not just "blobs" of people that we don't know. The person sitting next to you on the bus or walking down your street is a sentient being. Remembering that all beings have been your mother in one lifetime or another, you should bring all your relationships to the path of practice. Practice with awareness that we are all sentient beings. And when you say, "May all beings attain happiness and the cause of happiness," be sure that you are that cause.

The only way to do this is to generate a strong commitment, from this moment on, to transcend habitual attitudes of body, speech, and mind. Observe yourself carefully when relating to others. Make sure that your thoughts are pure; if they're not, bring the mind back and strengthen the purity of your thoughts. Be mindful that your speech is pure so that it doesn't harm others. Be mindful that the body is respectful, courteous, and sensitive to others. And as much as possible, reduce your attachments, needs, expectations, and hopes. Give them a rest—and give others a bit more space and time. Learn from observation. Observe others and don't make the same mistakes; observe yourself and don't repeat your own mistakes.

Contemplation

A mahayana meditator generates vastness and flexibility by bringing awareness to every experience. Instead of developing an overly structured or form-oriented approach to practice, integrate the essence of meditation into all your activities. Even if you are not a meditator and haven't heard many teachings, you're on the right path if you are developing genuine kindness and selflessness.

When I studied with my own teachers, we would attend to them and travel with them, and they would use every situation to remind us to generate an attitude of vastness. Seeing a beautiful flower while walking along, for example, one could immediately say, "May the beauty of this flower be experienced by all sentient beings; at this moment, may all beings wake up to nature and be able to see this." If one stops to take a rest, one could say, "Through my resting today, may all sentient beings have the chance to rest a while."

Or perhaps one might see something harmful. In India, especially in hot summer months, one often sees weak, hungry-looking bullocks pulling carts with very heavy loads. When they're not able to climb a steep hill, they are pushed and whipped, and one can see the wounds on their necks. Sometimes riding in the car with my father, we would get stuck behind one of these carts because the bull could not pull its load. And all of us sitting in the back would be saying, "How bad, how sad this is. What can we do?"

His Holiness Mindrolling Trichen would always instruct us: "At this very moment, truly take on to yourself the pain and suffering this animal endures. By recognizing this suffering, the mind is made tender. As you become aware of this very apparent suffering, which simply needs someone to look at it carefully, make this aspiration: 'May this animal's life and suffering be short. May the confusion, fear, and pain of this moment descend completely upon myself, and may the power of this aspiration make it fruitful.'"

What does it mean for an aspiration or prayer to be genuinely fruitful? For an aspiration or prayer to actually come true, there has to be some basis for fruition, some "hook." The hook is said to be the power of all the virtue we have ever accumulated and the power of our wish to generate absolute truth. This forms the basis for taking on such suffering. In this way we not only take on the animal's pain, we also recognize its inherent true nature as well as its causes and conditions.

So just as a good situation can be offered for the happiness of sentient beings, a bad situation can also be workable. Of course the best thing to do, if you can, is to help in the conventional sense. But the conventional help we give must deepen absolute truth in the mind. Then we will sincerely understand not only the conventional suffering, but also how this suffering is created by ignorance.

In situations like these, our teachers always advised us not to become dramatic. Yes, you can cry at a time like that. You can feel great irritation or anger toward the ignorance of the person causing such unnecessary harm. And you can know that this is the depth of ignorance to which a person—fully endowed with the potential for genuine compassion—can go.

We must also look at our own aggression. We may not beat animals, but we may display unceasing ignorance toward ourselves and those around us. If our actions still say mine and yours, right and wrong, good and bad, how genuine is our commitment to overcome ignorance? Does our speech still make gossip a priority as we try to keep touch with who's in and who's out, who's going somewhere or going nowhere, who's getting married and who's invited or not? Is there constant separation or dullness or laziness of mind?

Our refuge commitment will never bring any benefit if our actions don't accord with that commitment. Bringing awareness to every experience generates the vastness and flexibility of superior motivation. Then we are not just *saying*, "May I do this for all sentient beings," but actually including the beings we encounter. We are also more sensitive to the *sameness* of the suffering of all sentient beings—and of their desire for happiness. If we deepen our ability to work with inherent mind in every situation we meet, good or bad, we will know what we're talking about when we talk about "liberation from samsara."

So examine the actions of your body, speech, and mind carefully and reflect on the motivation behind your refuge commitment. The real question is not whether you take refuge as a samsaric or mahayana person, but whether your mind actually develops any real renunciation of self and genuine—not fabricated—kindness. Then we can look at whom or what we take refuge in.

Objects of Refuge

The object of our refuge depends on our motivation, which may be lesser, middling, or superior. There are two classifications: samsaric objects of refuge and objects of refuge beyond samsara. A mind that is still samsaric takes refuge in something within the world of samsara; a mind that is able to go beyond that takes refuge beyond samsara.

Samsaric objects of refuge are still not free from the effects of samsara. They are again divided into ordinary and supreme categories.

ORDINARY SAMSARIC OBJECTS OF REFUGE are mountains, forests, inanimate objects, powerful gods, nonhumans, kings, and so on. Taking refuge in them is motivated mainly by fear. In Bhutan, for example, we have a tradition of making many offerings to mountain and forest gods, mainly because when you go into these forests you can get very lost. And there are ghosts, spirits, and other consciousnesses to pacify. So once a year, people make offerings.

In Tibetan and even Buddhist traditions there are many such rituals, and many people take refuge in such things. This doesn't mean we literally prostrate and say, "I take refuge" in the forest or the mountain—although it could. It is the belief system of people who are trying to do good by relying on the mountain gods, water gods, and gods of the forest. We're all familiar with such rituals and traditions. It's essential not to denigrate such a view but to understand the intention with which we approach refuge. When we talk about ordinary samsaric refuge, we are looking at a conventional versus absolute view.

Samsaric refuge has nothing to do with the ignorance or wisdom, compassion or liberation of sentient beings. It's about the pacification of certain conditions to provide immediate happiness or temporary relief from some kind of fear. Taking refuge in an ordinary object for some immediate benefit to oneself or one's clan, tribe, or community is still an exhaustible refuge—and anything that can be exhausted is conventional or ordinary. It does not completely and permanently free us from samsara, cause and effect, or fear. When we make offerings to the harvest gods for a good harvest, for example, there is no absolute benefit. I don't know of any tradition that says, "May all ignorance be purified, may wisdom be attained—*and* may all harvests be good!"

A SUPERIOR SAMSARIC REFUGE would be taking refuge in the Three Jewels without fully understanding their essence. This is done by ordinary people like ourselves who are still motivated to save our skins. We don't want to make any mistakes or do anything wrong. We have devotion to the teacher, although we may not know why; we do know the situation is very precious and must be handled with care. And we don't want to do anything whose fruition is unknown. So with deep respect, we take refuge in the Buddha, Dharma, and Sangha. Again, we Tibetans are a perfect example of this.

Many Tibetans actually have no understanding of emptiness and absolute truth—nor do they wish to. My grandmother is a good example. Her son-in-law, His Holiness Mindrolling Trichen, is head of the Nyingma lineage and a great master, and she has lived around many other teachers. She doesn't, however, want to hear anything about fundamental absolute truth. Whenever we try to say anything about this, she says, "No, no, no, no. That mixes everything up." For her, her lama and daily devotions are enough.

This is superior samsaric devotion. We have our method, or form, for relating to the Three Jewels: Buddha was a perfect gentleman who lived 2,500 years ago and showed the path of Dharma—and don't try to tell my grandmother he didn't look just the way she thinks he did; Dharma is just the teachings and texts that have come down to us; and the Sangha is all the monks and nuns. We don't want to make any mistakes or create any negativity by not having faith or devotion. That's one way to take refuge.

It is possible to have genuine faith based on form along with a very profound understanding. Most of us, however—not only Tibetans—tend to have great faith and devotion to the things we like. We develop great fondness for our teachers and teachings and are firmly devoted to some actual existence and form. This is based on attachment.

Attachment provides us with something to feel good about and gives us a sense of security and protection. We think that because we're so devoted to the Three Jewels, our teacher, our *yidam*, or whatever, it will result in some kind of freedom from ignorance or suffering. In other words, it might lead to some personal benefit. From that point of view, we are still relating to a samsaric refuge, even though it's superior to ordinary samsaric refuge. Of course from a Buddhist point of view, the Three Jewels would be considered a bit more profound an object of refuge than mountains and forest gods.

The Three Jewels are said to be a superior refuge because they are not deceptive. Deception lies not in the object of refuge but in our motivation for taking refuge. It occurs when our intentions are selfish, when we act out of fear of losing our ego, our sense of "I." It occurs when we worry that all sentient beings but ourselves will benefit from our selfless acts: having given up so much, we'll be left with nothing and no one to take care of us. Taking refuge solely for personal gain or temporary relief of suffering changes something pure into a deception. Padmasambhava taught that no matter how profound or good, a samsaric refuge is exhaustible and only for personal gain. Therefore, we should take refuge in the genuine Three Jewels, which can completely dispel all ignorance.

THE OBJECT OF REFUGE BEYOND SAMSARA refers to the essence of liberation in the form of the Three Jewels. When they are correctly understood, the Buddha, Dharma, and Sangha are recognized in terms of their fundamental essence, nature, and activity. This is what it means to take refuge in an object beyond samsara.

When we take refuge in the Three Jewels as supreme objects of refuge, we are no longer seeking temporary relief of suffering but the exhaustion of all concepts. We're not settling for anything less than the complete exhaustion of everything false or fabricated—which would completely dispel the darkness of ignorance and generate primordial wisdom. We call this refuge "supreme."

We are still talking about the minds of practitioners and their different abilities. At first we recognize a conventional Buddha, Dharma, and Sangha; then the absolute Buddha, Dharma, and Sangha; and then the indivisibility of conventional and absolute truth. From that perspective we can look at the Three Jewels as objects in front of us, as objects of realization, and finally as objects of suchness.

We can also talk about maturation from the point of view of the hinayana and mahayana paths of practice. The hinayana path includes the *shravaka*s and *pratyekabuddha*s. Shravakas are motivated by beginning motivation and pratyekabuddhas by the medium motivation of the hinayana path of self-liberation—the path that most of us are on.

Depending on our maturation, there is also a slight difference in which of the Three Jewels we focus on or emphasize. A person taking refuge with the maturity of a shravaka meditator will tend to focus on the Sangha as the object of refuge. A pratyekabuddha will take the Dharma as the main focus of refuge. A mahayana practitioner will take the Buddha as the main refuge. The reason for this is actually reflected in the definitions of the words *shravaka* and *pratyekabuddha*."

The word *shravaka* means "listener," or "one who hears." As a shravaka, our practice consists mainly of really listening to the teachings—and coming to the conclusion that it's impossible to attain such a state of buddhahood. Our sense of ourselves is very ordinary: "I'm so ordinary I can't possibly imagine myself as a Buddha. I'll focus instead on listening to the teachings of the various Sangha teachers." Great importance is therefore placed on Sangha, which we view as a lineage of messengers from the buddhas. Because our main emphasis is on hearing the teachings, when we take refuge in the Buddha, Dharma, and Sangha, we rely mainly on Sangha.

As a pratyekabuddha, or "solitary realizer," we see that until we actually put the teachings into practice, we will never dispel the ignorance that creates cyclic existence. At the same time, we have no desire to be in community; our greatest wish is to practice in solitude. In this way we can abstain from unvirtuous actions and are in no danger of being distracted by others. To safeguard our personal liberation, we tend to go off alone. We rely only on the teachings that we've heard and contemplated— and when we take refuge in the Three Jewels, our emphasis is on the teachings of Dharma.

As a mahayana practitioner, we rely on the Buddha as our supreme refuge. Moreover, we aspire to become a buddha ourselves. We know this is the only way that all sentient beings can be liberated, all ignorance purified, and all wisdom accomplished. We recognize that the Buddha whose teachings we hear and put into practice is within us. It is buddhahood, the essence of Buddha, that needs to be realized as the only real freedom from suffering. We take refuge in the Three Jewels with Buddha as our supreme refuge—knowing that buddhahood is inseparable from ourselves.

The mahayana refuge can be divided into sutra and tantra depending, again, on our intention and object of refuge. We are still talking about the minds of practitioners and their different abilities. At first we recognize a conventional Buddha, Dharma, and Sangha. Then we recognize the absolute Buddha, Dharma, and Sangha; and then the indivisibility of conventional and absolute truth. From the mahayana perspective, we can look at the Three Jewels as objects of realization and objects of suchness.

SEEING THE THREE JEWELS AS OBJECTS OF REALIZATION, we recognize the Buddha as the indivisible essence, or form, of the three *kaya*s. The three kayas refer to the *dharmakaya, sambhogakaya,* and *nirmanakaya.* Dharmakaya means "the fundamental essence," sambhogakaya means "the nature of that essence," and nirmanakaya is the action aspect of the nature and essence together.

For example, we can look at the three different but inseparable aspects of the sun. The inherent essence of the sun is its nucleus; the nature of the sun is the fact that it's visible, glowing, and radiant; and the sun's action is to generate light and heat. These three things are indivisible and together they make up the sun. In the same way, the essence, nature, and activity of the mind are indivisible, and the essence, nature, and activity of the Buddha are indivisible. Moreover the essence, nature, and activity of the Buddha, the mind, and the sun are the same.

How is this so? It is so because in their essence, nothing can be found. In their nature, they may manifest in various ways as the sun, the Buddha, or the mind. And they may manifest various actions—good, bad, light, dark, warm, cold, whatever. Nevertheless, when the light and heat of the sun dissolve into their nature, and the nature dissolves into its essence, the sun is space. In the same way, the mind is space and the Buddha is space as well. This is a simple way of understanding pervasive essence, which is our fundamental essence.

The essence of the Buddha, Dharma, and Sangha is the very same as the intrinsic essence of mind. While this empty essence cannot be found and has no form, it is not a void or blankness; it is not like becoming unconscious or unable to react. There is still a nature, which is the ability to present something and the clarity of that presence. The nature of the Buddha is the clarity of knowledge or knowing. Our own inherently empty mind has the same clarity. If mind were empty in the sense of void, we could never recognize or know anything or even generate ignorance. The nature of the empty essence is the ability to know and the clarity of that knowledge.

The activity aspect is basically what we've become: the various forms of our bodies, activities, and responses. It's the container in which the essence and nature of mind manifest. The activity aspect of the Three Jewels manifests in the same way: the Buddha manifested 2,500 years ago as the teacher; the Dharma manifests as the body of teachings and practices; and the Sangha manifests with its compassion, guidance, and inspiration. This nirmanakaya, or action aspect, is also called compassion. So we have the compassion of the Buddha, the compassion of the Dharma, and the compassion of the Sangha.

When we no longer see the Three Jewels as distinct entities but as the indivisibility of essence, nature, and action, the Three Jewels are an object of realization.

TAKING REFUGE IN THE BUDDHA especially from the point of view of tantra, or vajrayana, we see that buddhahood is not about overcoming negativities or obscurations; it's about the complete exhaustion of concepts, or twofold purity. The Buddha, the supreme jewel, is endowed with the qualities of twofold purity, namely primordial purity, and the removal of all temporary obscurations.

Primordial purity means that the Buddha is no longer seen as someone who lived and taught 2,500 years ago—which is a very conventional or relative view leading to a samsaric object of refuge. Seeing the indivisible essence, nature, and compassion of the Buddha, we recognize the inherent primordial purity of the Buddha.

The second purity is the removal of all temporary emotional and wisdom defilements. Since primordial purity not only is inseparable from but actually manifests the Buddha, we see the indivisibility of absolute and relative truth. At this point, mind can finally let go of emotional defilements, which basically means grasping at any and all emotions. Obscurations arising as emotional defilements are purified or removed as we progress on the path.

Wisdom defilements are any slight hint of separation between self and others. We may be completely victorious over emotional defilements such as anger, jealousy, hatred, desire, or ignorance; nevertheless, the slightest separation persists when we continue to think we should manifest compassion for sentient beings. Out of limitless compassion, we still want to generate compassion toward others. An example of this is the story of Avalokiteshvara, one of the deities in the Tibetan vajrayana teachings.

Avalokiteshvara, the Lord of Compassion, is the manifestation of the compassion of all the buddhas. It's said that when he attained liberation, he saw sentient beings suffering in the six realms in great turmoil and pain. So, gathering together all the wisdom and merit he had ever accumulated, he made an aspiration to truly liberate all beings. And the six realms were emptied.

Avalokiteshvara was very happy—until he saw that the six realms had filled up again. Again he generated great compassion and emptied the six realms, and again they filled back up. He did this three times—but no matter how hard he tried, sentient beings continued to suffer. Because of the great pain and remorse of not being able to help sentient beings, his head split into a thousand pieces. It's said that when Amitabha Buddha joined all the pieces together again, Avalokiteshvara finally understood the karma of sentient beings. So compassion isn't just having an aspiration to help all beings, it's being able to recognize their karma.

This story shows how the slightest obscuration of wisdom mind can separate even a mature bodhisattva or meditator from sentient beings. As long as there is still something to do, something to attain or maintain, there's enough ground for everything to continue as it is—even *without* emotional defilements. This is what is meant by wisdom defilement, which is completely purified by the genuine exhaustion of all concepts.

Taking refuge from the point of view of tantra, we recognize that buddhahood is the complete exhaustion of concepts, or twofold purity. What is the exhaustion of all concepts—and what is *not* a concept? Samsara is a concept, nirvana is a concept, a sentient being is concept. The subject, the object, and their interactions are concepts. The helper, the one helped, and the act of helping are concepts. For ignorance to survive, any concept will do, spiritual or otherwise. Liberation, or realization, is the complete exhaustion of these concepts—good or bad, pure or impure. Recognizing twofold purity, we take refuge in the pure form of the Buddha as an object of realization.

TAKING REFUGE IN THE DHARMA OF REALIZATION, we recognize the indivisible essence, nature, and action of Dharma, which is absolute truth. Truth cannot be defined or colored. It's not conceptual or deliberate; it's the natural truth just as it is. The essence of the Dharma of realization is beyond expression.

We need to know what we mean when we say, "I take refuge in the Dharma." A beginner's definition of Dharma might be "truth" in the sense of T-R-U-T-H; but what about the rest of the alphabet? If Dharma is the body of the teachings, then what is not Dharma? And if everything is Dharma—even negative things—then when you say, "I prostrate to the Dharma," what are you prostrating to? Think about that. The Buddha taught that in degenerate times he would still be present in the form of written words. But is Dharma just written words and texts? It could be. Dharma is also "truth" in the broader and deeper sense: it is the pervasive quality that is absolutely pure and true.

The Dharma of realization is truth beyond expression in words and form.

Anything that obscures that truth is considered wrong view. A wrong view—anything that hinders, contaminates, or denies all-pervasive fundamental truth—is a manifestation of ignorance. Dharma effectively dissolves ignorance. It is the means to remove every stain of hindrance or false view so that inherent purity and truth can be realized. From this point of view, we take refuge in the Dharma of realization.

The nature of Dharma is the path of buddhahood, or practice. This is the path of hearing, contemplating, and meditating. It is based on knowing what we need to cultivate and to abandon. The path is the means to overcome obscurations of conceptual mind. The action or compassion aspect of Dharma comes to fruition through the practice of Dharma and the cessation of suffering.

Another aspect of the Dharma in which we take refuge is the scriptural transmission of Dharma. This refers to the oral transmissions of the Buddha and the commentaries of the great masters: the 84,000 tenets of sutra, Vinaya, and Abhidharma, and the four or six tantras. We relate to these scriptural transmissions not in a conventional way but from the absolute approach of realizing their essence.

From this point of view, we would see all written forms, including individual letters, as Dharma and respect them. We should never, for example, sit on or step over or be disrespectful of written forms. Many people, I'm afraid, have the bad habit of seeing only Dharma texts as Dharma: newspapers and magazines don't count. I sometimes sit and watch people jump over written practice materials. More knowledgeable meditators get very upset about this saying, "They're stepping over the Dharma!" But we must remember to look upon *all* written forms as Dharma, not just texts. When we talk about Dharma, we must understand the indivisibility of scriptural transmission and the Dharma of realization.

TAKING REFUGE IN SANGHA, from this point of view, refers to the great arhats, bodhisattvas, and all living examples on the path of freedom from ignorance, including all those who have at least gone beyond emotional defilements—and practitioners who possess these qualities, such as ourselves and those in the spiritual community. According to the lesser vehicles, anyone who has taken refuge and is on the path of practice is also said to be the Sangha jewel.

Causal and Fruition Refuge

CAUSAL REFUGE views the Buddha, Dharma, and Sangha as causes leading to our own fruition or liberation. The Three Jewels are supreme objects of refuge and examples of what we would like to become. By making an aspiration such as, "May I, through the support of the Sangha, walk on the path of the teachings and attain the same mind as the Buddha," we take Buddha, Dharma, and Sangha as causes for realization. So causal refuge refers to the object of refuge as the cause of liberation.

FRUITION REFUGE refers to our ability to realize that our own mind's essence, nature, and compassion are indivisible from that of the Buddha, Dharma, and Sangha. Therefore, the Buddha is the very essence of our own mind, Dharma is the nature of our mind, and Sangha is mind's ability to bring compassion and awareness to every moment. Recognizing the Three Jewels as indivisible from our own mind, we take the fruition refuge, which liberates our mind from ignorance.

Mind's indivisibility from the three refuges means that a completely purified mind—unstained and unfabricated—is the unchanging Buddha. That unchanging awareness, or vajra mind, is the Dharma. And from that awareness, we generate those qualities that best benefit others, which is the Sangha aspect. That is the fruition refuge: the completely pure Buddha.

The Tibetan word for the Three Jewels is *könchok sum* (*dkon mchog gsum*); *kön* means "rare," *chok* means "very precious or supreme," and *sum* is "three." So the Three Jewels are supreme and very rare. Taking refuge in the outer way, we can realize the inner refuge, the primordial purity of our own mind. The inner view of this supremely rare and precious treasure is our inherent basic goodness.

The Three Jewels are the object of our refuge because of their six jewel-like qualities:

1. They are extremely rare.
2. Their unstained essence is free from any fabrication.
3. Their power—which is the power to benefit by generating wisdom, compassion, and skillful means—is precious and supreme.
4. This preciousness is an "ornament of the world"—and anyone who takes refuge and remains within the commitment to absolute essence becomes an ornament of the world.
5. They are supreme. The meaning of the essence and nature of refuge is free from ignorance and is therefore supreme.
6. Taking refuge in the Three Jewels, we are able to realize an unchanging good and genuine heart.

The actual taking of refuge begins when, in an open and sincere way, we approach the preceptor and ask for permission. At this point, the teacher generally explains refuge and examines each person to determine if he or she is qualified to take the vows. Instructions are then given, and we must reflect on our ability to keep that commitment. If we are confident that we can do so, the refuge vows are given in a formal ceremony. The ceremony itself has three stages: again the explanation of refuge, the recitation of the refuge vows, and the giving of a name.

Having taken refuge, we might ask how long our commitment lasts. In general it's said that we take refuge from now until enlightenment. Actually, however, the duration of refuge depends on our motivation when we take refuge. For a person taking samsaric refuge, our commitment lasts from the moment we take refuge until our refuge aspiration is fulfilled. For someone with the motivation of a shravaka or pratyekabuddha, refuge lasts until our own death. For the mahayana practitioner, it lasts until all sentient beings attain liberation.

The Seven Benefits of Taking Refuge

Having said that we take refuge until all sentient beings attain enlightenment, we next consider the benefits of taking refuge. The seven benefits of taking refuge are actually seven kinds of qualities.

THE FIRST BENEFIT is that we are free from wrong view, which simply means a non-Buddhist view. Wrong view is not about theories; it refers to a view not in keeping with what Buddhism actually teaches: awareness, selflessness, and genuine compassion. This is what we mean by a Buddhist view. It is not really about Buddhism but about *truth*—basic human truth that can and should be developed from other traditions as well. It is the most profound intention and meaning of any philosophy or religion.

In the hands of human beings, however, religion is always being interpreted, in ways that are convenient for our group, culture, or tradition. Even Buddhist practitioners want things done a certain way. This personal interpretation is convenient to create and maintain because it suits our expectations; this is what we then value as Dharma. When buddhadharma is interpreted to fit our own expectations or style, it only leads to further entertainment—which is *not* a Buddhist view. We may call it Buddhism and spend a lifetime pretending we're doing the right thing, but nothing will make a false concept into pure truth. It is essential to know that holding wrong view means interpreting things with a selfish mind that likes to entertain itself.

A more traditional definition of wrong view is to be lacking in concern or awareness about harming others. This view finds no need to refrain from negative actions such as killing, stealing, lying, sexual misconduct, gossiping, covetousness, maliciousness, or harmful angry words. Jealousy, hatred, and the intention to harm others are not considered negative. Even if we are great

Buddhist meditators, monks, or nuns, if our actions indicate a careless attitude toward our character or conduct—no matter how stubbornly we insist that we're good practitioners with many vows—we're still holding wrong view.

In spite of our basic goodness, we can detour from awareness into habitual likes and dislikes. We may be lazy about accumulating virtuous actions or letting go of harsh speech, disrespectful attitudes, or harmful physical conduct. A lazy attitude is lacking in awareness. We simply go toward the easiest thing to do, say, or think, with no effort to be aware of our environment. If this is the case, then no matter how many teachings, practices, or dedicative activities we take part in, we are still holding wrong view. Wrong view should be understood in these various ways.

The main thing is to reflect on our actions. If our actions cause harm, it is similar to being born in a place where the Buddha's teachings have never been taught or heard. Taking refuge, we generate a strong commitment to awareness and become a Buddhist. The difference between a Buddhist and non-Buddhist is based on our refuge commitment. Based on the truthfulness of this commitment, we develop awareness of body, speech, and mind, which results in not holding the wrong view. This is the first benefit of refuge.

THE SECOND BENEFIT OF REFUGE is that our faith in the Three Jewels becomes the cause of not being born in the lower realms. The cause of birth in the lower realms is creating harm and unhappiness for sentient beings. At every moment our actions can create experiences similar to the diverse sufferings of the lower realms—or worse. Our actions might, for example, create a hungry ghost–realm experience of famine and poverty. We've all seen human beings in different parts of the world enduring terrible sufferings similar to the hungry ghost realm— along with all the human-realm sufferings of birth, old age, sickness, and death. When the cause of this suffering is dissolved, there is no such fruition.

Working with the refuge commitment, we cultivate the virtuous conduct of awareness and refrain from actions based on anger, attachment, or ignorance. In this way, our actions of body, speech, and mind not only don't harm, they actually benefit others. Now most of us experience some suffering— some greater than others—but we all have the precious opportunity of a human life. We may not know how long we'll live, but at least we have this moment. Moreover, we have met the teachers and teachings and we have a supportive Sangha, which creates a practice environment. All the circumstances have been made ready for us. All we need to do is actually begin to practice.

Contemplation

When you look deep into your heart and mind, how do you see yourself as a person? How truthful and flexible are you? How much of what you understand in theory can you put into practice? Your mind and tongue may talk constantly about benefiting sentient beings, but do you really care for sentient beings? How genuinely gentle and tender is your mind? Are you sensitive to the needs of others? How much awareness do you bring to your actions, so you don't harm another or take a life? Is there any indication in your speech of these tremendously positive causes and conditions coming together? Or are you lazy and unaware, slipping into habitual tendencies and—because of that slip—losing this precious opportunity? And how many times has this happened before? The fact that we're here now means that up until now we have let each moment slip away due to one emotion or another, one moment of unawareness after another. Surely now is the time to develop more awareness.

This life is the great fruition of many lifetimes of hard work: lifetimes of cultivating virtuous actions, abandoning unvirtuous actions, and accumulating good causes. To have arrived at this point where so many good causes and conditions come together is due not so much to the blessings of others but very much to our own hard work. This culmination of accumulated virtue and development of awareness has enabled us to overcome unvirtuous distractions and actions. In this precious lifetime the moment of fruition is now.

The fruition is each and every moment we encounter. The question is, will we actually work with this culmination of innumerable lifetimes of hard work, or will we let this pristine moment slip away? Although we carry an immeasurable treasury of conditions into this moment—virtue and accumulated merit, a human birth, motivation and commitment, teachers and teachings—we may let it slip away. And we may let the next moment slip away, and the one after that. Then we begin to understand what the Buddha really meant by the suffering of sentient beings.

Realization is very easy to attain. We simply need to choose to attain it. Each moment, there's a point at which we actually choose between nirvana and samsara. Nirvana, or enlightenment, is not something we attain only once, having gone through a series of practices one by one. It is ever present. It doesn't have to be searched for, bought, or conquered. Ultimate enlightenment is the closest thing to us—we just don't see it, just as we don't see our eyelashes. We only see what's more obvious and vivid "out there:" she, he, they, it; good, bad, long, short; mine, yours, and so on. Getting tangled up in that, we don't see the immediacy of this moment.

Samsara and nirvana are inseparable, and each moment has the full potential for both. Detouring into samsara, we continue to churn out an immense samsaric creation—and all of its suffering, the cause of which is ignorance. From the ignorance of not remaining in awareness, grasping and the endless creations of the six realms arise. With a genuine understanding of our refuge commitment, we see the importance of becoming responsible for our own karma. By decreasing unvirtuous actions, we exhaust the causes of being born in the lower realms.

THE THIRD BENEFIT OF REFUGE is that refuge establishes the ground for all further vows and precepts. Taking the basic five precepts, for example, we vow to abstain from killing, lying, stealing, indulging in sexual misconduct, or taking intoxicants. In this way we abstain from any actions that harm others through our conduct. Both lay and monastic precepts—even the 253 precepts of fully ordained monks and 364 precepts of fully ordained nuns—are based on the refuge commitment, without which we cannot take on other precepts or bodhisattva vows.

To say that vows cannot be taken on simply means that we must discern between experimenting with something and genuinely putting it into practice. We don't need to take a vow to experiment with these things. We don't need to tell anyone what we're doing, and no one will keep tabs on us. Actually taking a precept or vow means coming forward with a courageous mind that, rather than looking for entertainment, genuinely understands the *benefit* of these vows. Recognizing the value of maintaining the precepts and developing awareness of body, speech, and mind, we develop the courage to put them into practice. We are then measured in terms of our confidence, in terms of actually practicing awareness with courage and dedication.

The basis of all these vows and precepts is our refuge commitment. In the Tibetan Buddhist tradition, taking refuge is called "entering the gateway of Dharma." We are then qualified to participate in all levels of teachings and instructions, empowerments, transmissions, and explanations of texts.

THE FOURTH BENEFIT OF TAKING REFUGE is freedom from obstacles. Having taken refuge, we are said to be guided, supported, and protected by the Three Jewels—and therefore free from obstacles. We could compare this to taking a strong companion along when we go to an unknown place, someone who can help us and calm our fears. Recognizing the true essence of the Three Jewels and relying on them as a refuge provides us with support, guidance, and protection. They strengthen the mind—and weaken the mind's fear—in order to overcome obstacles. *Obstacles* here means distractedness, selfishness, habitual tendencies, and self-grasping. The power of refuge develops our awareness, which strengthens the mind so we can overcome distractions and habitual tendencies.

So, in times of need, refuge is said to dispel all obstacles. Just as we bring the mind back to one-pointedness in meditation, we can bring all distractions into one-pointedness by focusing the mind on the Three Jewels. We are so often preoccupied with the events of our lives. Emotional outbursts of sadness, fear, loneliness, depression, or disappointment distract us and weaken our commitment to practice. We begin to feel lazy and don't want to meditate. We no longer see the point of trying to be aware—and why should we think of others if nobody is thinking about us? With this kind of logic—feeling uninspired and discouraged on the path—we withdraw from the good things we're developing.

By reciting or just being mindful of the Three Jewels, we can strengthen our refuge vow and overcome obstacles. When we recite the refuge prayer, mind is supported by our speech. By physically joining our hands and visualizing the Buddha, Dharma, and Sangha—sensing their presence—we understand the essence, nature, and compassionate aspect of refuge. Then we can truly say, "Other than you, there is no one I can rely on or go to for protection."

THE FIFTH BENEFIT OF REFUGE is freedom from disease. Only the ultimate refuge—the ultimate Buddha, Dharma, and Sangha—brings genuine freedom from the sufferings of old age, sickness, and death. There is no freedom from these sufferings as long as we are working within samsara, creating the causes and conditions of suffering. Freedom from disease means that the foundation of refuge and the path of practice bring us to the ultimate realization of the exhaustion of concepts. Ultimate freedom from birth, old age, sickness, and death comes only through dispelling their causes.

If we really want to be free from the sufferings of birth, old age, sickness, and death, we must meet each moment completely within its potential for perfect freedom from all concepts. For this we must strengthen our practice by taking refuge so we can recognize the purity of this moment—and stop wasting our lives because of ignorance. This will bring freedom from the suffering of birth, old age, sickness, and death. Therefore, refuge is said to be the foundation of freedom from disease.

THE SIXTH BENEFIT OF REFUGE is purification. The texts explain how all previously accumulated karma and obscurations are purified, or completely exhausted, through taking refuge—which is quite similar to overcoming the causes leading to the lower realms. Purification means actually disciplining our body, speech, and mind so we don't slip back into habitual tendencies.

Having committed ourselves to strengthening awareness and clarity and overcoming habitual patterns, we put these precepts into action by taking refuge with our physical body. We willingly and with awareness refrain or pull back from physical habitual patterns. Taking refuge with our speech, we pull back with our speech so it doesn't display its habitual and unnecessary tendencies. The refuge commitment to train the mind brings the mind back so it doesn't deviate from awareness. We purify habitual tendencies of unawareness through the practices based on refuge, the foundation of awareness.

THE SEVENTH BENEFIT OF REFUGE is the accumulation of merit and wisdom. All of the teachings and disciplines for developing awareness of body, speech, and mind arise from the foundation of refuge. There is no other source of merit. The only way to accumulate merit is to develop awareness of body, speech, and mind. Merit is none other than that. So our refuge commitment is the basis of merit.

From this, wisdom arises. When awareness is clear and sharp and at all times awake, we understand samsara more clearly. We also realize how immediate and inherent nirvana is. That realization cannot be taught; we must see it and taste it for ourselves as it arises from the ground of awareness. For this we need a sharp mind, which comes from the strength of our refuge commitment.

Now, if mind is really that selfless, shouldn't it be easy to generate selflessness? This is true. But we're unable to simply dedicate our lives—body, speech, mind, and everything we love—to the path of selflessness. We need something to inspire us when our attachments and distractions are still so strong. We may turn to our intrinsic buddha nature for inspiration, or we may rely on our sense of how nice it would be generate "selflessness." Liking the comfort, support, and guidance this gives us, we decide that the right inspiration will enable us to go in the right direction.

Nevertheless, on the path of completely dispelling all concepts, we must realize how very attached we are to concepts, how very entertaining they are, and how very much we need them. The greatest attachment of all is to our own path of practice. We like being a "Buddhist practitioner." We like the comfort of meditation: the feeling after sitting in meditation is like a warm blanket on a cold night. When we spend two or three hours practicing —well done! Each concept is like a carrot in front of a donkey that doesn't want to run. Some clever person found that hanging a carrot in front of a donkey would help it win the race. So the donkey has his carrot for inspiration, and we have our if-you-do-this-you'll-get-that sense of fruition.

Now, this is not about donkeys and carrots; it's about having a conceptual reference point. For every conceptual cause, there's a conceptual fruition. So as long as we are *thinking* about emptiness, we have not realized emptiness. In this case, there's no need to be afraid—or not afraid—of it. Nothing has changed and nothing ever will. Until emptiness is actually realized, we still have our relative, conventional ground, our relative path, and relative fruition.

The ground of refuge, on the other hand, is meditation. Because of meditation, we have a genuine path of refuge. As our understanding matures and deepens, we become less preoccupied with concepts until ultimately they no longer entice us. When we develop a real sense of "groundlessness," concepts are no longer required. We spontaneously let go of grasping, and spontaneous selflessness develops. Everything that arises is natural and unfabricated beyond concept. Selflessness is not contaminated by ego or ego's ignorance. And it has no need for the comfort of fruition, because selflessness of ground creates selflessness of path and selflessness of fruition.

From that point of view, "benefit" is the natural ability to give rise to the fundamental truth of refuge and compassion. Whatever arises free from self-grasping is none other than genuine compassion. Compassion is no longer just a term, and it no longer needs a doer or action to be accomplished. But until we really realize the exhaustion of concepts—not just talk about it, but truly realize it—we are still working on conventional ground, with a conventional path leading to a conventional fruition. From that perspective, we can talk about the seven benefits of refuge. Next we will talk about the guidelines for maintaining that commitment.

The instructions for maintaining our refuge commitment can be explained in two ways: ordinary instructions and extraordinary, or particular, instructions. Ordinary instructions also have two categories: actions that should be abandoned and those that should be cultivated.

The Ordinary Instructions on What Needs to Be Abandoned

THE FIRST PRECEPT, from the moment we take refuge in the Three Jewels, is to abandon samsaric refuges and to cultivate selflessness and the path of practice. A samsaric object of refuge provides only temporary relief or fruition—a moment of happiness or freedom—for oneself alone. It is meant to save our skins or fulfill a particular wish or selfish intention. This doesn't mean that in keeping with a particular culture, custom, ritual, or event, we cannot show respect to such objects of refuge for others. We do not break our refuge vow by doing this, and it doesn't mean that such objects of refuge are improper. But we have to examine our mind and intention in taking refuge.

Refuge is about our most basic, innermost mind. It is something to which we can entrust ourselves—our very life, our soul, our consciousness—completely. We could say that by virtue of this trust we take refuge, and as a result of it we develop awareness and compassion. So taking refuge in the Three Jewels refers not to an object but to an absolutely true essence, which is our own true nature. Our intent must be to exhaust all ignorance and generate a genuine understanding of absolute truth. This is what we mean when we say, "I take refuge in the Buddha, Dharma, and Sangha."

THE SECOND PRECEPT is not harming others. Having taken refuge in the Dharma, we are immediately bound to be aware of our actions. No act should harm or hurt another, including those lower or weaker than us—human beings or any other form of life. We must not take another's life to sustain our own or in any way beat or enslave sentient beings or make them work for us. A person who has taken refuge must abandon as much as possible even the thought of harming or having selfish intent toward other sentient beings.

A THIRD PRECEPT is to avoid companions who hold wrong views. Having taken refuge in the Sangha, we should avoid the company of anyone who encourages such views, for example, that there is no harm in killing or hurting sentient beings or that there is no benefit in compassion. We should also avoid people who make discouraging remarks such as, "Only losers would put their effort into developing awareness." Any tendency to twist the teachings to suit ourselves or satisfy grasping at our favorite concepts or perceptions is a misunderstanding of Dharma. Even a person who is technically a Buddhist can indicate through words or actions that he or she has detoured from the path of awareness and kindness and would be considered a wrong kind of companion. Having taken refuge, we should stay free of such a person—with the understanding that it's not about the *person* but our commitment to the path.

We can look at these instructions from the point of view of our hinayana and mahayana practices—which is not meant to disrespect anyone but to be clear about the disciplines we should take on. When the mind is more susceptible to habitual tendencies, we are more impressed by outside influences that cause us to deviate from awareness. A practitioner of tantra, on the other hand, might see the situation as simply lacking in wisdom or skillful means. We might jump right in and try to work with such a situation. This path is meant for a person who has developed much courage, irreversible confidence in the path of practice, and an unshakable, mountainlike commitment.

You must know your own mind. This precept depends on the strength of your commitment to awareness. It may be so strong that it wouldn't deviate or be influenced by anything. At that point, you don't have to follow this precept. If you are truly unshaken by anything, then, as a true bodhisattva, you should work to transform every negative situation into something positive. But be very careful and, as much as possible, discern the people who misunderstand or misuse the Dharma.

I recently read a book that talked about attaining liberation without developing kindness—because kindness is just a concept. This is a very serious misunderstanding of the teachings. If we believed that, we would again be falling into the trap of ignorance, of simply not wanting to be kind. Without realizing it, such persons would still need praise, popularity, or personal gain. Hearing something good about themselves would make them feel happy, and hearing something critical would make them sad. As long as such concepts are at work, kindness—concept though it may be—is still very much needed.

So use all of your intelligence and common sense to acquire knowledge of the Dharma. Then use that knowledge to discern between right understanding and misunderstanding of Dharma. This precept needs to be maintained by anyone who takes refuge in the Sangha.

In the sutra teachings, a person who takes refuge in the Three Jewels is said to be a precept holder. The meaning of this can be expanded to mean "friend of virtue," which refers to awareness and the path of absolute truth. A friend of virtue is one who—realizing the importance of mindfulness of body, speech, and mind—abandons harmful actions and cultivates benefit for beings. Such a person is said to be worthy of prostrations and supplication, even from the gods.

The Ordinary Instructions on What Needs to Be Cultivated

Having taken refuge in the Three Jewels, the texts say, we need to cultivate respect. Even the tiniest particle of a symbolic representation of Buddha, the smallest portion of a written word of Dharma, or the merest scrap cloth representing the Sangha should command our respect. Having taken refuge in the Buddha, we should see any representation—a statue, painting, picture, or postcard—as a genuine representation of the Buddha. Any form of written word, even a letter of the alphabet written on the ground, should be seen as Dharma and respected as a real teaching. Just as we regard the text on the shrine as a sacred object, every book we own—even the pencils we write with and all the notes we take—should be regarded as the words of the teacher and respected as Dharma. The Sangha is represented by pieces of cloth in Dharma colors—shades of red, blue, and yellow. These colors refer specifically to the robes of monastic monks and nuns. When we see even a small piece of that cloth, we respect it as a representation of the Sangha.

We are talking here about objects of respect—and not more than that. It would make no difference if you turned your back to the shrine and sat facing the door. There is absolutely no one to say otherwise, is there? When the teachers die, they don't take our respect with them: students may *give* respect, but no one takes it. And there is no Buddha, Dharma, Sangha, protectors, or deities with tally books saying, "Oh, I see you didn't bow to me that time—therefore, you're going down to the three lower realms."

Relating to the Three Jewels with respect is a way of disciplining ourselves. If and when we see ourselves as practitioners of buddhadharma, we will encounter other practitioners and teachings and buddhas all the time. So the more supports and structures we have to remind us that we actually *are* practitioners committed to practicing awareness of body, speech, and mind, the better. We therefore take on the discipline of viewing all form, even a small stone, as a reminder. Traditionally, if one finds even a broken bit of a stupa, one would value it as much as the stupa itself. If one has a representation that one respects or actually prostrates in front of, one would treat even a photograph of that representation with the same respect. This reminds us of our commitment.

In this way we also develop impartiality. A mind that plays the game of being respectful in some circumstances and not in others, being aware on some occasions and not on others, or doing the right thing when people are looking and not so right when they're not is giving in to laziness. Everything should remind us to train the mind. Just as we pay respect to a sacred Dharma text, by the same token we don't devalue or demean our morning newspaper—or the words we've written ourselves. Why would we discriminate between the two? Only an untrained mind would show respect to those with shaved heads, those sitting on thrones, but not to others. This is "discriminating mind" in the untrained sense. If it continues, we will find some sentient beings more in need than others, some occasions when we are more mindful than others. This is one of the many ways in which habitual tendencies arise.

To train the mind, we must understand the sacredness of everything at all times. No one direction is better than another, because all directions are sacred. No one object is more pure, because everything is pure as it is. And no one person is better or needier than another. The interpretive mind constantly makes these judgments based on what we can get from them. Such discrimination influences awareness and envelops the mind in ignorance. Discriminating kindness is partial kindness; discriminating devotion based on likes and dislikes becomes partial devotion—until everything that arises is contaminated with ignorance. Train the mind instead to be impartial and aware at all times.

The Extraordinary Instructions

FIRST, no matter how beneficial or profitable it may be, never abandon your commitment to refuge—even at the cost of your life. If someone held a knife at your throat and told you to let go of your commitment or lose your life, what would you do? Think about it carefully. If you don't think you would hold to your commitment even at the cost of your life, ask yourself why you're not able to let go of attachment. Why is it still difficult to generate compassion instead of selfishness? So often we make lists of things to do: practicing Dharma may be high on the list, along with generating devotion, kindness, and compassion. But enlightenment may actually be low on the list. Having taken refuge, we must realize the value of our precepts and commitments. Then—no matter how profitable, comfortable, familiar, or pleasurable other tendencies may be—we will hold to that commitment.

Contemplation
Ask yourself how serious you are about generating selflessness and compassion and doing something to benefit sentient beings. How strong is your commitment to the path—especially if you have been practicing for many years? Is it truly more valuable than your life, more valuable than your sense pleasures and attachments? If you really want to understand absolute truth, it's essential to think about how honest you've been, how true you have been to the path of realizing absolute truth.

Absolute truth is there at every moment. Yet here we still are—with all our dedications, commitments, vows and precepts, devotion, compassion, methods of meditation, lineage teachers, and teachings—still unable to attain realization. This is simply because, in our heart of hearts, our Dharma practice still takes second place. We still want to do what we want. We still want to complete other projects. We still distinguish between loved ones and others and think in terms of this and that, mine and yours. Those causes and conditions continue to be important—which is not what the teachings mean by "letting go even at the cost of one's life."

THE SECOND EXTRAORDINARY QUALITY we should develop is the ability to remain in the refuge commitment at all times and in all activities. The instruction is—whether walking, eating, drinking, or sleeping—to try to develop a genuine sense of awareness of the Three Jewels as inseparable from your own mind. Abandon any distractions that cause your mind to deviate from the awareness of indivisibility, and cultivate this in all your actions.

Traditionally, in guru yoga and other practices, one circumambulates a stupa while taking refuge and visualizing the Three Jewels on the right shoulder. Going in a clockwise direction, every circumambulation is made to the Buddha and bodhisattvas within. To develop awareness, some teachers will always turn to the right when they get up, no matter which direction they want to go in. With a sense of holding the Three Jewels within, every turn to the right is like circumambulating a stupa. Even if you haven't received instructions for visualization, you can have a sense of the Three Jewels at all times.

This deepens our understanding of the indivisibility of the Three Jewels and the essence and compassion of our own mind. Wherever there is awareness, there are the blessings of the Three Jewels. Where there is no awareness, no matter how much devotion we have, there is not much benefit—some benefit, of course, but a very conceptual benefit. Having taken refuge, it is essential to develop awareness of the Three Jewels at all times.

These are the conducts to cultivate according to the extraordinary precepts. You should study them well. This will develop a more precise understanding of refuge. If you are planning to take refuge or have already done so, you really need a clear understanding of what refuge means. If you have not taken refuge, you can continue to work towards that. And remember that the ground of refuge is meditation; it is because of meditation that we have the path of refuge (see appendix A for basic meditation instructions).

Contemplation

Here are some other ways to remain inseparable from refuge.

- When eating a meal, begin with a sense of the Three Jewels at your throat. Then offer the first mouthful of food to them.
- In the same way, if you see or hear something beautiful, make an offering.
- If you see or hear something painful that rouses your anger, you can say: "This is aggression. As a person on the path of meditation, I recognize this aggression and offer this awareness to the Three Jewels."
- Sitting in meditation, sense the presence of the Three Jewels at all times.
- Repeat the refuge vows three times in the morning and three times before going to sleep to accomplish the six sessions traditionally done in retreat. Begin with a strong commitment to develop awareness of body, speech, and mind.
- At night, conclude by reaffirming that commitment and reflecting on how well you were able to maintain it during the day. Then, gathering together any benefit, dedicate that to sentient beings by reciting the simple refuge formula: "I take refuge in the Buddha, I take refuge in the Dharma, I

take refuge in the Sangha." Or compose your own simple refuge supplication.

* When sleeping, gather the essence of the Three Jewels in your mind and, with a sense of indivisibility from them, take that into sleep.

Often in our eagerness to go on to other levels of practice we don't work with what we have, which results in a weak foundation. The habitual tendency is to eagerly keep taking the next steps, but they too will be weak because the foundation is not strong. No matter how many practices we build upon it, mind will remain the same: hard, rigid, and fixated. So it's essential to work completely and thoroughly with what you have.

It is also important not to look at refuge as merely a beginning step. In Tibet, teachers like Atisha emphasized the refuge teachings and practices so much that refuge alone was all one needed to practice. Try to see the wholeness of the practice and commit to really understanding and strengthening it. Then taking refuge will not just mean getting a name; it will become a complete foundation for all the teachings of the Buddha.

Now we have spoken about turning to refuge—in spite of obstacles such as ill health—as a source of strength and continued commitment to the path. And we have seen the importance of *not* turning to samsaric remedies in times of suffering. So how should we actually confront physical or emotional difficulties? Should we rely only on the remedies of mantras, meditation, and practices that strengthen our determination and motivation? Or should we turn to the advice of physicians, psychologists, and the support of other therapies to enhance our physical or mental health when necessary?

The answer is that we should continue to exert effort in our practices. This doesn't mean, however, that we cannot engage in other forms of recovery or rely on expert diagnoses and advice.

Any recommended methods or medicines that enable us to strengthen body and mind can be seen as inseparable from the teachings and instructions of the Buddha. These methods, too, can be ways of cutting through our opinions.

Very often in the East, instead of going to a doctor for a remedy, people go to a teacher for a divination when they have a terrible headache or they're unable to sleep. Here in the West, there are those who think pain will strengthen their practice, who take pride in not caring for themselves. This goes against the path of all practices and fails to acknowledge the preciousness of human life. In order to dispel this tendency, these instructions have been given in the texts.

We all want to meditate well and attain some kind of fruition. We all have good intentions and want to do good. Nevertheless, we tend to separate ourselves from our practice: our life and identity on the one hand, our Dharma practice on the other. Separating our practice from our life, we tend not to trust it. Then we try to make them coexist like a marriage, but that doesn't work. The hesitation that arises from this false separation results in the feeling that sometimes we are Dharma practitioners and sometimes we're not.

If we have hesitation at the beginning of the path, we will not reach the state of enlightenment because we will lack the willingness to move forward. To reach enlightenment, we must cut through every level of hesitation. At this moment, when the fruition of our efforts could ripen completely, it is important not to permit a single neurotic behavior or strong emotion to distract us and dismantle all of the good karma we've accumulated. Hesitations arise at every point along the way and we resist taking the final step. Keep in mind from the very beginning that we've come a long way to be where we are today. It would be very unfortunate to hesitate now—yet this is what most of us do. Fear of groundlessness keeps some of us from taking the next step. Others resist because of fear of the unknown: what would happen if we let go of the self?

I find it amusing when people say they will believe in enlightenment when they've attained it. The path of selflessness is constantly obstructed by hesitation or doubt. The very pith of Buddhist practice—and the very reason we practice—is to go beyond that hesitation, which is nothing more than an empty thought empowered by our energy. In and of itself, it has no structure, no reality, and no potential to germinate or arise as an obstacle. Holding on to this thought, however, we give it the energy to transform into something dangerous, fearful, and big. We could spend a lifetime succumbing to the energy we put into otherwise empty thoughts—which would be a waste of this precious human life.

This moment is the fruition of the many lifetimes in which you have struggled to be a good person, to walk on the path of right and abandon things that are wrong. The courage, determination, and renunciation that you have developed so far are tremendous. To dedicate your life to practice when there are so many other things that you could do is one of the greatest offerings you can make to the Three Jewels. It is also one of the greatest acts of generosity that you can extend to sentient beings.

Contemplation

Contemplate your life and who you are as a person—especially your great capacity for goodness. Think of all the hard work and all the teachers, buddhas, bodhisattvas, Sangha, and teachings that continuously generate the blessings that have brought you to this precious moment. Contemplate the fruition of this moment so that when you leave your meditation, you can really say, "This is what I would want to give to sentient beings."

From the Buddhist perspective, we must recognize the effort that we've made to get this far—and be aware that this journey never ends, even at the point of enlightenment. Don't settle for anything less than this. From the moment you enter the gate of the Dharma, work on this commitment with confidence and complete honesty. Our practice will not truly be honest until we are genuinely motivated to reach enlightenment in one lifetime and to benefit all sentient beings. This is the way enlightenment expresses itself—as unbiased, all-pervasive compassion that benefits all beings.

What would it take to really achieve this? We cannot achieve enlightenment and unbiased compassion by "doing it my way." This only creates attachment to the forms or formulas we particularly like. Wherever attachment arises there can be no freedom from illusion or selfishness and no absolute truth. So as you practice and study, hold in your heart these two aspirations: to benefit all beings and to remain within the understanding of absolute truth. This is the view we should hold and hope to attain.

Concluding Dedication

M AY THE MERIT gathered here—past, present, and future—benefit sentient beings. May the path of practice
continually develop awareness of body, speech, and mind. And
may that luminosity dispel the darkness of ignorance in the
minds of all sentient beings. Furthermore, may this form the
foundation of a strong path leading all beings to the accomplishment of the mahayana. As they conduct themselves in accordance
with the teachings and instructions of this path, may the merit
and virtue of all sentient beings be the cause of happiness for all.

APPENDIX A
The Practice of Meditation

Hearing, agreeing with, and having devotion to Dharma will not benefit anyone unless the Dharma is actually applied in meditation. Otherwise we are like a physician who dies of sickness or a treasurer who spends his time counting money and dies in poverty.

Meditation practice in the Buddhist tradition is about "changing your mind," which means transcendence of mind. When the ordinary mind goes from a state of ignorance to awareness, absolute truth can arise unimpeded by the sense perceptions. This is the intention of meditation practice.

There are two types of meditation: shamatha and vipashyana. The ground of shamatha is a peaceful state free from concepts. When we shift into distractions, shamatha provides a reference that supports and strengthens the ground of awareness and brings the mind back. Focusing the undistracted mind one-pointedly permits a genuine understanding of the true nature of whatever arises. This wisdom of discernment is vipashyana meditation, which analyzes and recognizes the true nature of all inner and outer phenomena.

In the beginning, it's difficult to recognize and develop awareness because of constant distractions. Our mind and body must be trained. Because of the physical, gross body, we're continually distracted by and grasping at grossness. The body is the container of meditation and must be tamed and trained to remain still. Within stillness we can recognize the difference between useful and useless movement—and realize our potential for resting in awareness.

The meditation posture trains both the body and mind—both of which are inherently empty in nature. Body and mind are joined by the breath, or wind element, which is called *prana* energy. Wind energy is the closest thing to space. Since the space quality of mind and body is the same, we can understand the truth of the slogan "Training the wind energy trains the mind." The body is trained through the wind energy, and wind energy is trained through shamatha meditation.

The traditional meditation posture is known as the seven-point posture of Vairochana. This posture disciplines the body so the flow of prana is more subtle and clear and less impeded. When the body supports the wind and wind supports the mind, these three form the foundation on which mind can be quickly trained.

Basic Meditation Posture

To begin your meditation practice, you can use this very simple approach to the seven-point posture:

1. Sit on a soft cushion on the floor with your legs crossed. If you can, sit in the full- or half-lotus posture. In full lotus, both feet rest on top of the thighs, with the soles turned up. If this is too difficult, sit in the half-lotus posture, resting one foot on the floor under the other leg, and the other foot on top of the opposite thigh. If you have knee or back problems, sit on a chair. In order to have good concentration, it's important not to be in pain. The crucial thing is that your spine is straight.

2. Place your hands in one of two contemplative gestures. Placing your hands palms down over your knees straightens the hands and the flow of wind energy in the body. The second, more traditional way is to cradle the back of your right or left hand in the palm of the other hand, with both palms up. The thumbs are touching to form a lotus or jewel. Position the hands four finger widths below the naval, resting on your feet or touching the thighs and abdomen, with the tips of the thumbs almost at the level of the navel. It's essential for the energy in the hands to flow, so the body needs to be straight. If this posture is too difficult, or if you have long arms and hands, place your hands on your knees.

3. The spine should be as straight "as an arrow piercing from the apex of your head down to your seat."

4. The shoulders are also straight, pulled back but relaxed, with the arms parallel to the sides of the body, "as an eagle ready to take flight."

5. The chin is tucked in gently toward the Adam's apple. The neck is therefore slightly bent but not too tight. This chin position helps to straighten the spine.

6. The tip of the tongue should touch the front of the palate or the base of the front teeth.

7. The eyes are open and the gaze flows down the slope of the nose to a point directly in front of you. Take that point as a support for maintaining mindfulness. Maintain the posture with your eyes open. Closing the eyes only *seems* to facilitate practice; it brings only temporary one-pointedness. The eyes are the main gateways of distraction and need to be trained. Otherwise distractions will arise when your open your eyes.

Three Preliminary Steps to Meditation

Begin your meditation session with these three simple preliminaries: first, generate a sense of strong commitment; second, generate genuine devotion to the Three Jewels by taking refuge; and third, dedicate your practice for the benefit of all beings by generating a strong sense of bodhichitta.

By generating compassion and devotion to the teacher and the Three Jewels, we become genuinely aware of the essence that should be taken into meditation. Everything we have talked about up to this point is contained in these three simple steps.

Basic Meditation Technique

In shamatha meditation, the gaze is especially important. Using an external object—a pebble, stick, statue, or candle flame—can temporarily free the mind from disturbances and distractions. Together with the posture, concentrating on a focal point in front of you allows the one-pointedness of shamatha to arise. When the mind is still, try to remain in that stillness and strengthen it. When the mind shifts, go back to the beginning. If one-pointed focus creates a sense of dullness, sleepiness, boredom, or laziness, relax the gaze. One antidote is to lift the gaze upward, then allow it to slowly come down.

You can also develop one-pointedness in "formless" shamatha by focusing on the breath. When meditation is more stable, training the breath is especially useful. Taking your posture, dissolve the six senses on the in-breath and bring awareness to the out-breath. If it's difficult to let go of grasping at distractions, you can begin by counting the breaths. One-pointed concentration is developed by allowing the mind to actually mingle with the breath.

Rest the mind completely in whatever arises. For example, if a thought arises, label the thought "thinking" and let it go. Labeling thoughts and letting them go is using the thought as a reference for one-pointedness. You could also label any sight, sound, and so on—and just leave it at that. Rest the mind without elaborating with adjectives like good or bad, perfect or imperfect, great or small. Do not analyze, interpret, or judge. In this way, take whatever arises as the reference for one-pointedness.

When the resting mind becomes distracted, there are two ways to bring it back. The basic antidote is to breathe in and allow the mind to settle again. Another way is to come back by allowing whatever has arisen to dissolve. This antidote is like throwing a pebble into a lake and letting it sink, becoming one with the lake like a drop of water. In the same way, recognize any thought that arises as a distraction and allow it to sink, becoming inseparable from settledness.

Your practice sessions need not last too long. Begin with short frequent sessions. In shorter sessions, we are able to identify the gap, that small, still moment of complete dissolution of concept. Sitting regularly for even ten or fifteen minutes is a good way to begin. If you can sit for forty minutes or an hour a day, that is good, but it doesn't have to be all at once.

Keep in mind that various instructions for meditation need not conflict with one another. There are many suitable methods. The important thing is to find one that works for you. Basically, shamatha meditation can be done in any posture. You can sit on a *zafu* and *zabuton* or sit on the ground if you have no cushion; you don't need a certain kind of cushion to get your shamatha done. The important thing is your mindfulness-awareness meditation. If a certain posture is helpful to your practice, do shamatha in that posture. If you have difficulties with a certain posture or set of instructions, you can work with it.

Meditation practice is a journey. We begin in a very deliberate way, and as our confidence grows, we can relax. The most important thing for beginning your meditation journey is to find someone qualified to give you instruction and to clarify your questions. See appendix B for resources for further training.

APPENDIX B
Resources for Further Practice and Study

SINCE 1999 TO 2002, Khandro Rinpoche has conducted an annual Gateway Program in Baltimore, Maryland. These intensive training seminars continue to be offered in various locations as an entry to the Buddhist path. Mahayana and vajrayana teachings are also offered internationally. For more information about Khandro Rinpoche and her teaching activities, please see the web site: www.mjkr.org.

To learn about other centers offering Tibetan Buddhist teachings, see the following web sites: www.shambhala.org and www.kagyu.org.

Information regarding Buddhist postsecondary education can be found at www.naropa.edu.

Bibliography

Recommended Reading

Gampopa. *The Jewel Ornament of Liberation.* Translated by Khenpo Konchog Gyaltsen Rinpoche. Ithaca, N.Y.: Snow Lion Publications, 1998.

Longchen Yeshe Dorje, Kangyur Rinpoche. *Treasury of Precious Qualities.* Translated by the Padmakara Translation Group. Boston: Shambhala Publications, 2001.

Patrul Rinpoche. *The Words of My Perfect Teacher.* Translated by the Padmakara Translation Group. Boston: Shambhala Publications, 1998.

Further Reading

Dakpo Tashi Namgyal. *Mahamudra: The Quintessence of Mind and Meditation.* Boston: Shambhala, 1986.

Jamgon Kongtrul the Great. *The Teacher-Student Relationship.* Translated by Ron Garry. Ithaca, N.Y.: Snow Lion Publications, 1999.

Shantideva. *The Way of the Bodhisattva.* Translated by the Padmakara Translation Group. Boston: Shambhala Publications, 1997.

Thrangu Rinpoche. *Buddha Nature.* Translated by Erik Pema Kunsang. Kathmandu: Rangjung Yeshe Publications, 1988.

Wangchug Dorje. *The Mahamudra: Eliminating the Darkness of Ignorance.* Translated and edited by Alexander Berzin. Dharamsala: Library of Tibetan Works and Archives, 1978.

Yeshe De staff. *Ways of Enlightenment.* Berkeley: Dharma Publishing, 1993.

Tibetan Texts Referenced

Lochen Dharmashri. *Chab dro yenlag drugpay chü jang zinmatik zhugso [Skyabs 'gro yan lag drug pa'i bskyud byang zin ma tik bzhugs so]. Commentary on Vimilamitra's First Discourse on The Six Stages of Refuge*

Jigme Lingpa. *yon tan mdzod* (Skt. *Guna Kosha*). *Treasury of Knowledge*

Glossary

Tibetan terms appear first in phonetic rendering and then in transliteration.

ARHAT One who, through hinayana practices, has gone beyond emotional defilements to attain the lesser fruition of individual liberation, or "arhatship."

AVALOKITESHVARA (Tib. *Chenrezig; spyan ras gzigs*) One of the deities in the Tibetan vajrayana teachings, known as the embodiment of compassion.

BODHGAYA From *bodhi*, meaning "awakening," the actual place where the Buddha attained enlightenment and first taught. Also known as Vajrasana, "land of vajra," or "vajra mind," referring to buddha mind or a situation or place where, upon viewing vajra mind, one could realize one's inherent buddha nature.

BODHICHITTA (Tib. *jangchub sem; byang chub sems*) "Awakened heart" or "enlightened mind." It relates to the mahayana principle of loving-kindness and genuine compassion, the generation of which cuts through selfishness and dispels the ignorance that grasps at individual liberation.

BODHISATTVA A fully enlightened compassionate being who, through the "superior" motivation and practices of the mahayana path, goes beyond personal liberation to benefit all sentient beings. (See also Three yanas)

DISCURSIVE THOUGHTS (Tib. *namtok; rnam rtog*) Concepts arising from habitual tendencies. They undermine confidence in enlightenment but can be recognized in meditation as mere tricks of the mind.

EIGHTEEN QUALITIES (Tib. *daljor choje; dal 'byor bco brgyad*) The basic qualities of a precious human existence, composed of the eight freedoms and ten endowments.

EIGHT FREEDOMS (Tib. *dal-je, dal brgyad*) The freedoms that make it possible to bring one's human existence to fruition. The first three refer to freedom from birth in the three lower realms. The fourth is freedom from birth in a barbarous place; the fifth, freedom from birth in the god realm; the sixth, freedom from wrong view; the seventh, freedom from birth in a place without a buddha; and the eighth, freedom from being born deaf and mute.

FOUR REMINDERS Four preliminary instructions known as the Four Thoughts That Transform the Mind: the preciousness of a human birth, impermanence, the suffering of the six realms of samsaric existence, and karma.

HINAYANA. *See* Three yanas.

IRREVERSIBLE CONFIDENCE The confidence that comes from recognizing and being sure about the presence of one's core essence of enlightenment; it brings willingness to train the mind and is connected with devotion.

KALPA (Tib. *kalpa; bskal pa*) An eon lasting for thousands of years and made up of four stages: origination, continuation, gradual disintegration, and complete extinction.

KARMA Any cause, or first action, producing some effect or fruition, which then becomes another cause. Awareness of cause and effect brings understanding of karma.

MADHYAMIKA SCHOOL The Middle Way teachings of Buddhism, which expose the falsity of the extreme views of nihilism and eternalism.

MAHAYANA. *See* Three yanas.

MILAREPA (1040–1123) Great yogi and poet of Tibetan Buddhism and the Karma Kagyu lineage.

NAGARJUNA (2nd cent. C.E.) Indian philosopher/dialectician and originator of the Madhyamika school.

NIRVANA One of the many names for enlightenment, it refers to removing ignorance that obscures the mind and realizing absolute truth.

PRANA ENERGY The wind element, or breath.

SAMSARA (Tib. *khorwa; 'khor ba*) That which spins, or moves in circles, referring specifically to the cycle of suffering.

SENTIENT BEINGS (Tib. *drowa; 'groba*) In Tibetan, literally, "movement," signifying the presence of a mind or mental consciousness, and a holder of that mind. The immense amount of movement in the realms of samsara is created by beings with bodies and minds, all of whom desire happiness.

SHAMATHA MEDITATION (Tib. *shine; zhi gnas)* One-pointed state of "calm abiding," allowing one to remain in the uncontrived ground of awareness.

SIX REALMS The three lower realms (hell realm, hungry ghost realm, and animal realm) and three higher realms (human realm, jealous god realm, and god realm) of samsaric existence. Since the god and asura (jealous god) realms are often considered as one, the six realms are sometimes referred to as five realms.

STUPA A form of sacred architecture representing the pure presence of the Buddha and embodying essential principles of the body, speech, mind, qualities, and actions of enlightenment.

TANTRA(s) (Tib. *jud; rgyud*) The vajrayana teachings given by the Buddha in his sambhogakaya form. Tantra, meaning "continuity," refers to the expression of innate buddha nature in tantric scriptures. Tantra can also refer to all the resultant teachings of vajrayana as a whole.

TEN ENDOWMENTS (Tib. *jorwa chu; 'byor ba bcu*) The five individual and five circumstantial endowments of a precious human birth: (1) in a human body; (2) in a "central place"; (3) with senses intact; (4) with right view; (5) with devotion, or irreversible confidence; (6) with the Buddha having been born in this kalpa; (7) with the Buddha having taught the Dharma; (8) in the presence of the Dharma; (9) among practitioners of the Dharma; and (10) with compassion in the hearts of the teachers.

TEN UNVIRTUOUS ACTIONS The three unvirtuous actions of body (killing, stealing, and sexual misconduct); four of speech (lying, sowing discord, harsh speech, and idle chatter); and three of mind (covetousness, wishing harm on others, and wrong view). Their opposites are the ten virtuous actions.

TERDAG LINGPA (1646–1714) Also known as Minling Terchen Gyurme Dorje, an incarnation of Vairochana and one of the greatest Nyingma lineage holders and discoverers of hidden teachings. He was a teacher/disciple of the fifth Dalai Lama and founder of Mindrolling Monastery in central Tibet.

THREE JEWELS (Tib. *könchok sum; dkon mchog gsum*; Skt. *triratna*) The Buddha, Dharma, and Sangha in whom one takes refuge.

THREE KAYAS Three "bodies" of realization—dharmakaya, sambhogakaya, nirmanakaya—connected with mind, speech, and body of existence. Dharmakaya refers to the "body of reality," or fundamental essence; sambhogakaya to the "body of complete enjoyment," or nature of the essence; and nirmanakaya to the "emanated body," the action, or compassion, aspect of nature and essence together. The indivisibility of the three kayas is the *svabhavikakaya,* also referred to as the "essence body."

THREE POISONS Attachment, aggression, and ignorance, which arise from basic duality and the initial clinging to a self.

THREE REALMS The form, formless, and desire realms are the three basic manifestations of samsara. Human beings are born into the desire realm, which expresses itself as the six realms of existence.

THREE YANAS The three vehicles of the Buddhist path. Hinayana, the "narrow vehicle," refers to an initial stage of self liberation, with an emphasis on cutting through ego fixation. Mahayana, the "great vehicle," brings realization of emptiness and egolessness of self and others, culminating in the bodhisattva path and the aspiration to liberate all sentient beings. Vajrayana, or "indestructible vehicle," sometimes referred to as "tantra," recognizes wisdom and compassion in the form of the guru, devotion to whom brings enlightenment, the fruition of the Buddhist path.

TONGLEN (Tib. *tonglen; gtong len*) Literally, "sending and taking," a contemplative practice that generates loving-kindness and compassion for sentient beings.

VAJRAYANA. *See* Three yanas.

VIPASHYANA MEDITATION (Tib. *lhag thong; lhag mthong*) From the ground of awareness stabilized by shamatha meditation, vipashyana (insight meditation) arises as the wisdom of discernment that recognizes the true nature of all inner and outer phenomena.

YIDAM (Tib. *yidam; yi dam*) The energetic or expressive aspect of enlightened mind in the form of a tutelary deity. In Tibetan Buddhism, the focus of one's formal practice might be one of hundreds of such deities. As tutelary deity, the yidam is a personal protector of one's practice and guide to enlightenment.

Editor's Acknowledgments

THE EDITOR WOULD LIKE to acknowledge the many people who helped bring these precious teachings to the printed page. These include an indefatigable group of recorders and transcribers too numerous to list. Further appreciation goes to Jetsün Dechen Paldrön for ongoing assistance and support; Eugenia Pickett for the essential compilation and editing of initial materials; Dr. Karl Gross for ready assistance with several parts of this project including Tibetan literary references; Mary Bartley, Jeanne Ellgar, Deborah Kaetz, and Bonnie Rabin for careful reading of the manuscript and thoughtful suggestions; Scott Wellenbach for assistance with Tibetan translations; Mary Pat Brygger for logistical assistance; William Dintzis for technical assistance; Jann Jackson for valuable contributions to the final draft; and Emily Hilburn Sell, from beginning to end, for a sense of form worthy of the content.

Index